Bolivar, the Liberator

SIMON BOLIVAR

Painted in Lima by Gil, 1825

BOLIVAR
THE LIBERATOR

BY

MICHEL VAUCAIRE

TRANSLATED FROM THE FRENCH BY
MARGARET REED

With Illustrations

Boston and New York
HOUGHTON MIFFLIN COMPANY
The Riverside Press Cambridge

The Riverside Press
CAMBRIDGE · MASSACHUSETTS
PRINTED IN THE U.S.A.

TO
BLAISE CENDRARS
WHO LOVES A DANGEROUS
LIFE

'A creative genius *par excellence*, he drew his inspiration from the void. Always great, he was yet greater in adversity. A conquered Bolivar, said his enemies, was more to be feared than a conquering. Reverses lifted him above himself.'

O'LEARY, *Memorias*

PREFACE

A REPUBLIC, a province of Colombia, the largest port on the Orinoco (Angostura) — a whole tribe of towns and villages to-day bear the name of Bolivar. His portrait appears upon the stamps of several countries. All over the world there are streets called after him. There is a gold coin called Bolivar, and a kind of hat. During the 'glorieuses' of 1830 the Parisians sang a hymn in praise of Bolivar upon the barricades. If Miranda had his name inscribed beneath the Arc de Triomphe in the list of heroes compiled by Napoleon, in 1832 Bolivar's profile, modelled on a medallion by David d'Angers, was in the gallery of great men.

Few have attained to such glory as did Bolivar.

In France to-day historians of the highest repute, writing of Bolivar, are betrayed into the most deplorable of errors.

The wars of emancipation in South America were not brought about by rebellion of the natives; they were civil wars between Spaniards — Spaniards from Spain against families established in America for several generations and tired of European government.

Bolivar, the great hero of the independence of those provinces known as Tierra Firme, belonged to a very old Spanish family.

Space will not allow me to quote in full the letters and speeches of this man whom they called the Napoleon of South America. Many of the 'Libertador's' writings are rather lengthy, but a very complete collection of documents relating to the national hero has been published in Spanish in Venezuela. It fills no less than thirty-two volumes.

ILLUSTRATIONS

With the exception of the portraits the illustrations are from *Historia de la Casa de Bolívar*, by Vicente Lecuna and Julio Planchart, (Caracas, 1924)

BOLIVAR, THE LIBERATOR

I

VIENNA in 1804.

Winter.

In a commonplace hotel bedroom, in an unfamiliar setting, Bolivar felt that he was about to die. He did not fear death; on the contrary, he waited and hoped for it. How could he have expected to recover from his terrible sorrow? Why had he left Caracas? Coming to Spain in his impetuous youth, far from his own people, he had married at nineteen, and then had wished to take his young wife to America. Maria Teresa had died as soon as she arrived there. Alonso was right, when he discovered that country, in calling it Venezuela — poor little Venice. Now Bolivar had no hopes left in anything. He had wandered from one country to another, no town could hold him for long. Even his tutor and confidant had not given him the sympathy and encouragement that he expected. Rodriguez had merely said to him:

'Enjoy yourself. Mix with people of your own age. Go to the theatre and distract your mind. That is your only cure.'

As if he were capable of enjoying himself! To whom could he turn if Rodriguez failed him? Bolivar had come to Vienna solely to ask for his advice; but

his friend had taken a post as assistant in the labora-
tory of an Austrian nobleman, and now thought of
nothing but his work; Bolivar was less to him than
chemistry.

How dismal this house was! What time was it?

Bolivar felt the fever grow upon him. He threw off
his blankets. He was forgotten. He was afraid of the
coming night which he must spend alone and sleep-
less. He wanted a pen and paper to write to his
cousin in Paris, she had seemed to understand his
griefs; but she was married, she could never be more
to him than an affectionate friend, and that would not
make him forget Teresa. He could only see her at
balls, at soirées, in the middle of a crowd of men that
he detested. . . . What was the use of considering all
these follies now? Nothing but death could release
him from his troubles.

It grew dark. Motionless upon his bed, Bolivar
waited; he had fancied that he heard a step upon the
stairs, but no doubt he was mistaken. No one stirred.

It had been snowing. Bolivar saw the white roofs
on the other side of the street, and the snow reminded
him how far he was from his own country. What
were his brothers doing, and his mother? Bolivar
shut his eyes. He saw again La Guayra, from whence
you reach Caracas by the steep Cordillera roads; he
saw all the sun-scorched coast, the creepers on the
rocks, the waterfalls, the great lizards basking on
the ground; in the villages men in broad-brimmed
hats playing their guitars upon the doorsteps, with

brightly coloured *ponchos* over their shoulders; long-haired Indians, *aquadores*, their legs dangling as they sat backwards on their mules and used the tails for whips, skins full of fresh water swinging on either side; half-naked Indian women strolling along the path in the shade of the rubber trees.

Bolivar wept for this country that he would never see again. He wept for his careless childhood on the plains, among the tilled fields, the immense *haciendas*, the cattle branded with his family mark.

He fell asleep.

When he awoke he saw beside him Rodriguez and a stranger. They were looking at him and talking together in German. Bolivar was not strong enough to sit up. He listened without grasping what was happening.

The man bent over him, examined him slowly and shook his head; from time to time he turned toward Rodriguez and said a few words, then shook his hand, and nodding to Bolivar, went out. The tutor sat down upon the bed and fixed him with his eye.

'Simon, I am ashamed of you. I do not blame you for your grief, but I cannot say much for your courage. It is just such a test as this that should bring out your stoicism, and you let yourself go down at the first touch of sorrow.'

He went on with his scolding, but his voice softened; he explained the folly of wanting to die before you had really lived, he pointed out that love was not the only thing in life. Simon might yet be happy;

there was a difficult moment before him, but in such moments a strong character stands out; one must have some ambition.

Rodriguez spoke for a long time. He regained all his former influence over his pupil, and gradually he persuaded him that he must make an effort.

It was morning when Rodriguez went away. Somebody brought coffee and rolls. Bolivar ate mechanically. He no longer knew what he ought to do. He felt the influence of his master and submitted to it. He had not strength to resist.

The following night Rodriguez came back. All day Bolivar had been exalting himself with the idea that he might consecrate his life to some important work. His imagination ran away with him and he dreamt of devoting himself to some great project. But in his tutor's presence his enthusiasm waned.

'Certainly I see the attraction of a splendid future, but what can I do without money? I am poor, ill, a broken man. Better to die.'

'Saved! He is saved!'

Rodriguez sprang to his feet, his face kindled. Trembling with emotion he seized Bolivar's hands.

'If you were rich you would consent to live? Speak, answer me!'

He persisted, and Bolivar, astounded, did not know what to answer.

'Simon, are you child enough to believe yourself poor? You have never bothered to question it seriously. You have lived without considering your possessions; whatever your family sent you was enough and you were too proud to go any deeper. It seemed to me that you were right; I have always, myself, despised riches as a shameful frivolity, but to-day they have their uses. Your father owned valuable silver mines; he never told you about them because he felt that you were too young to understand their importance. Your father is dead; you have inherited the mines. You are old enough now to handle them. These mines are worth at least four millions. When you go back to Venezuela, your guardian will let you know the exact position. When you left Caracas after your wife's death, we saw that you were thinking of anything but money, and we decided to wait before telling you of your inheritance.'

Bolivar was overwhelmed with joy. He could at last give himself up to study, make discoveries, perhaps become famous. He yielded to the charms of his unexpected fortune. For an instant he feared that his tutor might be deceiving him, but on looking back he remembered sayings of his father to which he had not given much attention, but which now were clear.

He got up and dressed. He was stifled in that room with its elaborate furniture, its heavy hangings, its tasteless pictures; the room was still too full of his despair. He wanted to go away at once.

Simon Bolivar was one-and-twenty.

II

BOLIVAR flung his money about. In Vienna, in London, in Madrid, and in Lisbon he led the life of an aristocrat. He was lavish. He wanted at all costs to distract his mind, and was ready to squander his money at the first hint of pleasure. Naturally he at once became the prey of a circle of adventurers and lick-platters who flattered him and called him Prince. Bolivar let himself drift and grew bored. He played faro and lost a hundred thousand crowns in an evening. His tutor remonstrated, and Simon excused himself by saying that he had not been prepared for wealth and that so much money at once had gone to his head.

He came back to Paris, bought thoroughbred horses, expensive furniture and trinkets, and took a flat in the rue Vivienne; he went into society, never missed a good play at the Français or the Comédie Italienne, learned the catchwords of the day, made the acquaintance of a set of young Creoles who thought of nothing but amusement, ordered fashionable clothes, had several mistresses, and got himself talked about.

One night, as he was strolling in the Palais-Royal, he was accosted by a pretty, well-dressed girl who took him home with her to the rue des Bons Enfants. Simon did not try to resist. In the morning she said to him: 'You are Spanish?'

Bolivar was annoyed at the question.

'Where do you come from, then?'

'From Caracas.'

'Where the deuce is that?'

'In South America.'

'Is it pretty there?'

Bolivar described his home to her. All of a sudden he was proud of his town, of his estate, of his cattle and his mines which a month before he had not heard of; he spoke for a long time and with so much warmth that the girl besought him to take her there.

Tallish, with an olive skin, straight nose and bright eyes that were set off by long black lashes, a little moustache, thick hair and curly whiskers that hung on either side of a thin oval face, Bolivar put every one else in the shade; wherever he went he attracted all eyes.

Elegant, full of spirit, he could tell Creole stories, legends that pleased the young ladies; he danced well and was invited everywhere.

His cousin Fanny, whom he called Teresa after his wife, would have preferred him to take things more quietly. She dreamed of being his confidante, from whom he could hide no secret. Bolivar sometimes felt that she was right, that he was losing his time and squandering his energies; he was doing no work, but led an idle existence which occasionally sickened him.

Fanny, who had married M. Dervieu de Villars,

had one of the most brilliant salons of the day. There one met M. Récamier, Mme. de Staël, the Vicomte Lainé, the de Lameth brothers, General Oudinot, Eugène de Beauharnais, Humboldt, Talma, and Chateaubriand, who had just published 'René.'

In spite of his youth, Bolivar took part in every conversation, astonished people by the boldness of his ideas and fascinated them by his personal charm. He was the handsome, rather mysterious foreigner who might be pardoned for opinions that were witty but often daring.

He continued to gamble, gave gay dinners at his flat in the rue Vivienne, gave and received presents, rode in the Bois de Boulogne at the proper times, went hunting in the neighbourhood of Paris, and fought a duel, but not a serious one.

Bolivar was bored. He left the rue Vivienne for more modest lodgings in the rue de Lancry; he began to listen to his cousin when she reproached him for his useless life; he went every day to visit the savant, Alexandre de Humboldt, who had just made a journey of nine thousand leagues in South America, the most noteworthy exploration of that day. Humboldt had stayed with Bolivar's family and was still touched by the charming welcome that they had given him. He spoke feelingly of Caracas. Bolivar listened with respect, and looked at the maps which the explorer had made of regions hitherto unknown.

Humboldt asserted that the Spanish colonies were

advanced enough to govern themselves, but where was the man capable of leading them on such an enterprise? A friend, Bonpland, prophesied independence in the near future. Bolivar was enchanted. Humboldt told about the reception which had been given for him one Twelfth Night by one of Simon's cousins. His was not one of the dull and dirty houses of which South America can show so many, where the feasts invariably consist of a sheep roasted whole, from which each guest cuts his slices and eats it with his fingers, sitting on a horse's skull; no, this was a fairy-tale palace, an immense park as well cared for as those at Versailles, with fountains, statues and ruins like those of a picture by Hubert Roberts, a sumptuous feast and dazzling women.

Bolivar offered half of his fortune to Humboldt to found a College of Science at Caracas. He began to work, bought books, devoured 'L'Esprit des Lois,' and tried to fill in the gaps of his too scrappy knowledge. He perceived that the Rousseau-Rodriguez system of reading in the great book of Nature was not enough to make a man learned.

Humboldt had not forgotten the young Creole naturalist, Caldas, who unaided had been able to make instruments that were marvels of precision. He extolled the cleverness of the American race, and Bolivar was proud of it.

A story which his nurse had often told him came back into his mind. The priest who baptized him had refused to give him the name of Santiago which his

father had chosen, and had insisted on replacing it by
Simon, declaring that he had a presentiment that they
would one day see this child become the Simon Mac-
cabæus of the New World. The family had laughed
and given in.

Bolivar pictured a glorious destiny for himself.
Already he saw the Spanish yoke flung off and the
newly freed nations thanking him for his good offices.

He recalled the way in which he had been arrested
and beaten in the middle of the street in Madrid, and
that his resistance had only earned him an order to
leave the town; and all because he was rather friendly
with the Queen's lover. Bolivar detested this oppres-
sion.

When Napoleon was crowned Emperor, Bolivar
refused to be present at the ceremony. He could not
pardon this hero for himself becoming a tyrant.

He shut himself up in his own house and vowed
that he would not leave it, but there came up to him
from the street the clamour of the people, the songs,
the music, the rejoicings of Paris. Bolivar leaned out
of his window. He saw the crowd still cheering Napoleon as they returned, women shouting for joy,
impromptu dances at the street corners. All that was
gay in the greatest of capitals made festival to glorify
the name of a single man, and Bolivar in spite of himself envied him such fame.

III

Bolivar needed a change of air. He was pale; late nights, gambling, and excesses had made him thin. Rodriguez persuaded him to go with him to Italy.

They went on foot like a pair of friends, they would walk for hours, knapsack on back, and rest in the villages. It was the month of April, and it was pleasant on the roads of France. Bolivar could not keep himself from little adventures on which his tutor turned a blind eye. When they were very tired, they would ride in a peasant's cart. Simon admired this country so different from his own, and its painstaking farmers whom he saw for the first time at close quarters, who worked in the fields as long as it was light, and lived without much ambition, leaving a humble farm from father to son.

Rodriguez sometimes stopped at the side of the road to gather flowers or plants which he examined with a magnifying-glass, and whose family he expounded to his pupil.

This healthy life did them good. They were happy. One night they slept on straw, and Bolivar when he woke dipped his head into fresh water. He looked at his preceptor, who was sleeping peacefully, and could not help admiring this astonishing man, who eight years before had been at the head of a conspiracy to proclaim a republic and work out a constitution. Rodriguez had only escaped death by a miracle, and

since then he had lived in Europe, earning his living
without troubling over the future, changing his name
when the fancy took him, calling himself Robinson
after he had read Daniel Defoe; sometimes chemist,
sometimes a teacher of languages, never complaining,
knowing Rousseau by heart, an unlucky genius, a
soft-hearted adventurer.

Bolivar found a great mongrel dog, starving and
dirty; he took it with him and called it Carlos. The
dog became attached to him and followed him for
some time. One day it disappeared. Simon delayed
his departure from a little town in the hope of finding it, but search was in vain. The thing rankled in
Bolivar's mind for two or three weeks; Rodriguez
laughed at his sentimentality, but he too regretted
the dog.

The two men walked like this for four months.
They came to Italy and visited Milan, Venice, Ve-
rona, Padua, and Ferrara; they saw the march past of
sixty thousand French soldiers at Montechiaro. They
went as far as Naples, where they were the guests of
Humboldt's brother, who welcomed them with touching friendliness. Bolivar made the acquaintance of
Sismondi, of the German sculptor Rauch; he met
Mme. de Staël again. At Rome he stayed at the
Spanish Embassy, whither his reputation as a man of
fashion had preceded him; he was presented to the
Pope, and, to the scandal of the onlookers, he refused
to kneel and kiss the Pontiff's slipper. Pius VII,
however, smiled placidly and asked him for news of

South America. The story was told all over Rome, and Bolivar was invited to the houses of the Italian patriots. At one reception he declared that Bonaparte had lost a great deal by becoming Cæsar.

One day in the middle of August, Bolivar went for an excursion with Rodriguez into the environs of Rome. Simon had taken in his pocket the 'Æneid,' and the 'Annals' of Tacitus; from time to time he took out a volume and read it aloud as they walked.

It was overpoweringly hot, but the travellers took little account of it. They were pleased to find at last before their eyes the ruins of the greatest of civilizations. They came back in the evening when the sun was beginning to sink. They turned towards the Monte Sacro, and arrived sweating at its summit. The sky was red; before them they saw Rome. They sat down upon a block of marble, the last remnant of an ancient column. Rodriguez was tired; he could scarcely recover his breath; but Simon seemed wildly overwrought; all at once he rose, and, stretching out his hand toward the city and gazing at all those grass-grown monuments, he began to speak in a tone of deepest solemnity:

'Behold the capital of Romulus, of Remus, of Numa, of the Gracchi, of Horace, of Augustus, of Nero, Cæsar, and Brutus. From their countless tombs I see rise a distracted multitude of these great figures; but for one Cincinnatus, for one Trajan, for one Vespasian, how many Caracallas, Caligulas, and Claudii! Empresses, saints, courtesans, martyrs, priests, apostles, the blessed and the bandits, ghosts of crimes, of vices, of self-denial or of heroism, you have done nothing or next to nothing for humanity. What have you left to others except your names? What you have not been able to do, another will do for his country. On my honour and on my life I swear that this arm shall never rest until it has delivered America from the yoke of the tyrants!'

At that Rodriguez sprang up. Here at last was his pupil as he had always longed to see him. Sooner even than he had dared to hope, this youth, who a few months before had had no thought but to die of love and grief, had realized his part and had risen to it magnificently. Rodriguez was proud. He flung himself into Bolivar's arms and the two men embraced.

They returned slowly towards the town, turning over a thousand plans in their minds. As soon as possible Simon would leave this Europe with which he had nothing to do, and go back to the native land that needed him.

IV

BOLIVAR did not go as soon as he could have wished. He had been ill; the doctor who attended him, and to whom he confided his intention of making a long sea voyage, had flatly forbidden it.

Bolivar waited at Naples, and the time seemed interminable. He was expecting money which did not come. Rodriguez had gone to seek his fortune elsewhere. He wrote once from Constantinople, speaking of his pupil's great projects as if they were almost accomplished, and his enthusiasm was not enough to restore Simon's morale.

Moreover, the winter was not a good time for sea voyages; one heard stories of storm and shipwreck, and the sea was riddled with pirates who boarded without ceremony those ships that the elements had spared.

When spring came, Bolivar, recovered from his illness, thought of embarking at Bordeaux, but he could not leave Europe without once more seeing the cousin who wrote him such charming weekly letters. He decided to go by Hamburg and to pass through Paris.

Fanny, in tears, implored him to stay longer, but Simon's will was unbending. He promised to return; he was in earnest, he had regained all his confidence, and he knew that nothing could make him forget his duty toward his country, not even the cousin whom he loved better than he would admit.

Fanny realized that her prayers were useless. She had hoped to see Simon a strong and virile man and he had become one; she could not oppose his resolution, but she would have liked to keep him with her a little longer. Their farewell was touching. Simon went away so exalted by the greatness of his aims that not for a moment did he think of grief. Fanny had provisions brought for his voyage, saw to the details of his baggage, gave him books, a miniature of herself, and mascots, but she was inconsolable.

Bolivar reached Hamburg very quickly. The boat left for Boston next day.

Bolivar explored the harbour, which has been compared to the open jaws of a crocodile, with shelter for a fleet behind each tooth. He inspected the enormous warehouses and thought of the bay of Maracaibo at Cumana, whose industries he thought of developing. The ship in which he was to sail was a fine fourmaster, half equipped for commerce and half for war; she carried forty guns. Simon congratulated the captain upon her good order, and on the beauty of the carving at the prow.

While the ship was making ready, Bolivar thought of Fanny, and suddenly the wish came to him to go back on his decision. He looked at the miniature which she had given him; had he even thanked her for all that she had done for him? But would she ever pardon the weakness of such a precipitate return, would she not laugh at his short-lived dreams? Simon would not go back until he had done something; he would return famous. He choked back his tears.

He was interested in the working of the ship; the captain, who was Dutch, told him that in his youth he had bought negroes in Guinea to sell again in the West Indies; in the end he had been ruined by pirates. In those days he had only commanded a little brigantine of no account. Now he no longer feared any one, and he showed Simon how the guns were loaded. The crew was composed of experienced seamen who had seen more than one fight and had dealt in every kind of trade; they were of several nationalities: Irish, German, Scandinavian, Breton, and even half-naked Africans who climbed up the masts like monkeys.

Bolivar strolled up and down the bridge smoking; he read the 'Nouvelle Héloïse' and the 'Henriade'; he read also the novels of Nicolas Restiv and the younger Crébillon.

The weather was calm, the ship sailed steadily and the passage was as peaceful as could be.

One afternoon, when he had gone into his cabin to arrange the many things which he had brought from Europe, Bolivar came across his Freemason's diploma. He unrolled the great printed sheet, which showed a curtain hanging in an antique temple. It bore the different symbols, level, trowel, square, compass, the three points and the mallet, also crouching sphinxes. Bolivar recalled his introduction to the Lodge at Cadiz, whither he had been drawn by curiosity rather than conviction. He had taken oath to accept no legitimate government in his country save one elected by the free vote of the people, and to strive with all his might to establish a republican system.

He laughed over the Masonic ceremonies in which he had taken part, and where he had met too many tricksters and not enough fanatics. In Paris he had been raised to Master. Take it altogether, this association, with its childish airs of mystery, might yet have a practical use. He replaced the certificate at the bottom of a trunk and thought no more about it.

In the United States he saw pioneers working courageously, houses being built, and towns growing. He stayed for several weeks in Boston, which amazed him; the buildings in various-coloured bricks, the carefully paved streets, the enormous public buildings and the Exchange Coffee House, which contained two hundred rooms. Bolivar strolled along the Mall, a place of wide lawns intersected by avenues of trees.

He went on foot to Charlestown, the navy yard of which was famous. He saw an enormous man-of-war on the stocks. He compared his own country, still uncivilized, crushed by taxes and oppressed by Spanish governors, with this free, active, and ambitious nation. A small trading ship which called at La

Guayra took him at last towards the shores for which
he had so often longed.

How changed was his home! He heard on arrival
of his mother's death; his brothers had retired into
the country to look after their estates. Bolivar felt
himself a stranger in Caracas, but not for long. The
old friends of his family fêted his return, and in their
houses he had to retail everything that he had seen.
They questioned him about Paris, and about General
Miranda, whom he must have met there, and who
had just made a disastrous attempt to land on the
coast of Venezuela. Simon astonished them by his
elegance and the fineness of his clothes; he had seen
just what everybody wanted to see. Little by little he
renewed the associations of his childhood.

While he was in Europe several attempted risings
had miscarried; d'España's plot had been put down
with marked cruelty, and the leader's bleeding head
exposed in an iron cage. Captain Francisco Javier
Prela and ten of his friends had been sentenced, almost without proof, to imprisonment for life. The
least sign of rebellion was so severely suppressed that
any movement appeared impossible.

Bolivar was forced to postpone his schemes, which
seemed suddenly to have become extremely hard to
carry through; and besides, he was so much occupied
with his own affairs and with his success among the
women that he almost forgot his oath upon the Monte
Sacro.

Frenchmen were quietly eating their breakfast, began
to insult them, and threw stones at the door. The
officers went on with their meal unperturbed. As the
noise continued, they leant out of the window and
calmly contemplated the people in the square. Their
behaviour silenced the rioters. Profiting by this lull,
the Frenchmen left the inn by a door which led into
another street and went to the house of one of their
compatriots, a leather merchant.

The secretary Bello hastened after them and explained to them the danger to which they were exposed, informed them of the proclamation of fidelity
to Ferdinand VII, and persuaded them to leave as
soon as possible. At this point a sailor arrived and reported that a seemingly hostile British ship had just
anchored opposite La Guayra. Commander de La-
manon gave Bello a letter to the Captain-General in
which he said, 'I trust that you will not tolerate the
presence of Englishmen in this country.'

On the way back to their ship, the Serpent, the
officers passed the Englishmen, who had just disem-
barked, and, in order to avoid saluting them, they
turned away their heads and pretended not to see
them. Unluckily the wind had dropped and the Serpent could not sail. It was not until the next day that
she could take advantage of a slight breeze and get
under way. The English frigate at once gave chase.
At ten o'clock she was just within range and let fly
with her whole broadside. The Frenchman set her
studding-sails and went off on the port tack. How-

ever, a shot had cut the flag halyards; the Commander ordered the colours to be hoisted again at once amid shouts of 'Vive l'Empereur.' The mainmast was smashed just above the foretop, and the stays of the mizzenmast fell. The engagement was hopelessly lost and the Serpent had to haul down her flag and drop the port anchor. The English boarded her and took possession of the ship's papers, put a crew on board the brig, and took her into Trinidad.

The French expedition had come to a sad end.

Napoleon's envoys were very ill received in all the colonies of the New World. Meanwhile, the Junta at Seville despatched emissaries to announce the declaration of war with France and the failures of the French in Spain.

The enthusiasm was wild. There were public thanksgivings and everybody cheered for Ferdinand VII, of whom a month before nobody had heard. *Te Deums* were sung, and hats broke out into cockades of red ribbon on which were written in letters of gold, 'We will conquer or die for our King Ferdinand VII.' If Ferdinand had come to the New World, he would have had a triumphal reception. At Santa Fé de Bogotá the women stripped off their jewels and sent them to Seville to help on the war against France; fabulous sums were collected, and Creoles gave as much as four hundred thousand piastres for the 'good cause.'

VI

CARACAS is a town of forty thousand inhabitants. They are of all sorts, Indians, negroes, half-castes, and Creoles. At every step you come upon great mangy dogs. The streets are irregular, some of them wide and all badly paved. The jutting roofs are tiled with red, the windows painted blue or green, the walls washed with ochre or lime, and upon it all the sun beats down incessantly.

The people live in shirts and white trousers; only in the evenings do they dress themselves with care, put on polished shoes and expensive panamas. It is the hour for visitors. They sit on wicker sofas or lie in hammocks, while amid religious silence the mistress of the house plays sentimental tunes upon the spinet. When the heat grows less, they dance.

In the low quarters of the town, not far from those no-man's-lands where black vultures called *gallinazas* feed themselves on filth, there are hovels whose beams stick out like spurs. Linen is hung out to dry on them, and baskets of fruit. The roofs are covered with palm leaves. In the centre of the town the *casas altas* have a second story with a balcony; you enter by a passage paved with a mosaic of black-and-white pebbles and the knuckle-bones of sheep. There is always an inner courtyard where rain-water and mosquitoes meet. The rooms look out on this *patio*.

Bolivar gave a great dinner in his own house. There

FAÇADE OF THE BOLIVAR HOUSE IN CARACAS

were his brother Juan Vicente, the Toros, José and Martin Tovar, José Felix Rivas, Luis Rivas, Davila, Salias, G. Pelgrón, Rascio, Vicente Tejera, Nicolas Anzola, Lino de Clemente, the brothers Ayala, and Listaritz. They were the richest young men in Venezuela. The feast was magnificent, the cooking faultless, and the table was admirably decorated with baskets of flowers. When the slaves had cleared away, Bolivar had the doors shut and the conversation became more free; they talked of independence, and of the effigy of Miranda which had been burned in the market-place of Caracas by order of the Viceroy. A letter which that same Miranda had just succeeded in getting through to the patriots was read aloud.

'Spain has no longer a king; she is divided into parties, some devoted to France and others to England, and each one hoping to attain its own selfish ends by means of a civil war. The colonies are ripe for self-government; send agents to London and together we will work out the best means to assure the future of the New World; but no undue haste; one piece of imprudence might compromise everything. Lack of union would be death to our schemes.'

There was an emotional moment after this was read. A man stood on his chair and drank to 'Independence,' and all the guests thought of Miranda.

Born on the 14th of June in 1756, at Caracas, Miranda had left the country when he was seventeen; there had been question as to his father's claim to nobility. He went to Spain and covered himself with glory in an expedition against Algiers. Being then entrusted with a secret mission to Havana, he was accused of treachery by an officer jealous of his success. He sent in his resignation and took service with the United States, where, exalted by ideas of liberty, he fought under Rochambeau. Of gigantic stature and built like an athlete, Miranda was born to command. He went to Russia, where Potemkin presented him to Catherine. The Empress took an interest in this magnificent foreigner and made him a colonel. Frederick the Great invited him with Lafayette to watch the manœuvres of his grenadiers.

At the outbreak of the French Revolution he hurried to Paris to offer his services. They placed him, with the rank of field-marshal, on Dumouriez's staff. He was the hero of the retreat from Les Islettes and the first to enter Antwerp. When Dumouriez turned traitor, Miranda refused to march on Paris.

'You will fight against me, then?' Dumouriez asked him.

'Yes, if you fight against the Republic,' answered Miranda.

Dumouriez went over to the enemy and Miranda was brought before a court-martial. There could be no doubt as to his good faith; he was unanimously acquitted and received many congratulations; but the affair annoyed him; he retired into the country and bought an estate. His friendship for the Girondins brought him into bad odour at the time of the Terror; he was arrested and spent eighteen months in prison at La Force. After the death of Robespierre, he was released. He owned four houses in Paris which were a refuge for exiles from the New World.

Dining with a celebrated courtesan, Julie Ségur, the favourite of Talma, Miranda made acquaintance with Bonaparte, who was charmed with the spirit of the Venezuelan. Miranda had a finger in every plot. He was condemned to be transported to Cayenne, but escaped and took refuge in London, where he advised the Prime Minister to detach the American colonies from Spain. He produced a plan of attack, a constitution, and a commercial treaty. The English were amused at the restless giant, who was always ready to shake the universe, and who waited for hours in the lobbies, haranguing people in his strong foreign accent.

Since once more he had nothing to do, Miranda went to Egypt, where he made a living by various means. On his return after five years, he found England threatening to break with Spain, and he regained confidence. Pitt gave him an audience and listened to him, but deferred British intervention, having still in mind the reverse at Porto Rico.

After twenty different plans of campaign, Miranda was no further forward. The spies of the Spanish Legation had tracked him to London and his life was no longer safe there. In France the Directory had fallen, so he decided to return to Paris. He succeeded with some difficulty, and scarcely had he arrived when, at the request of the Spanish Legation, he was imprisoned in the Temple on an accusation of spying and stirring up sedition in the interests of the enemy. He was not released for some days, and then only on condition that he would never again enter the republican territories.

He went back to London, and his plan for the annexation of the South American colonies was given a favourable hearing, but England was herself so seriously threatened by France that trans-Atlantic affairs fell into the background.

Miranda landed at New York in 1805 with money borrowed here, there, and everywhere, and with Jefferson's approval he armed a two hundred-ton corvette, the Leander, under Captain Lewis, Armstrong second in command. They had two hundred men, eighteen heavy guns, forty field-pieces, fifteen hundred muskets, lances, and ample ammunition. The frigate L'Empereur was to have accompanied the expedition, but the captain broke his word. They had to be contented with two schooners, the Bacchus and the Bee.

Opposite Ocumare the flotilla was attacked by powerful Spanish men-of-war; the Leander could escape only by throwing all her ordnance overboard.

In despair Miranda found refuge at Grenada. He took heart again and got together a new fleet of ten ships. A French pirate sank one of his finest boats.

The landing in Venezuela was deplorable.

Meeting nothing but abandoned villages, hostile inhabitants, and disease, while the discontent of his

men became day by day more exacting, Miranda had
been obliged to leave this Venezuela which he had
believed to be more patriotic than it was.

The young men told this story as they smoked their
long cigars.

Simon Bolivar sat thinking in a corner. He was
the calmest of all. They even accused him of being
nothing but an amateur, useful enough in providing
money, but incapable of a personal effort. He thought
of Paris, of Vienna, of the Monte Sacro; what was to
be done with these men who talked so big and whom
the least check would overthrow, the least distraction
would divert, from their magnificent schemes? Ah, if
every one were as obstinate as Miranda, Venezuela
would soon be free!

It was late. Every one went home to bed.

VII

Wrapped in their many-coloured *ruanas*, barefoot, with big hats pulled down over their ears, incessantly spitting on the ground and ready to fuddle themselves with *guarpo* until they could not stand, the common people took no matter of interest in any political movement. One loved the King as one believed in God; he was too far away — nobody wanted to discuss him.

After the events of July, 1808, it was considered that Captain-General Don Juan de Casas had not shown sufficient presence of mind or firmness at the time of the French officers' arrival. It would have taken very little to make him recognize the usurper; he was courteously replaced by Don Vicente d'Emperán, a peaceable man, well disposed towards every one, virtuous and generally esteemed.

The Venezuelans soon got used to his leniency. They developed such a taste for it that, as soon as a moderately severe order was made with regard to illegal publications, the Liberals grew angry.

In vain did Emperán invite the most prominent members of this party to his house and there endeavour to argue them into a renunciation of their foolish ideas; they replied that a war with Spain was the only scheme worth thinking of. That was too much. Emperán had two or three of the leaders arrested and advised the others, among whom was Bolivar, to go and spend some time upon their country estates and not to set foot again in the capital.

On the 17th of April, 1810, came the news that Cadiz had fallen into the hands of the French.

On the 19th of April, the Liberals decided to seize their opportunity. It was Holy Thursday and all Caracas was going to the cathedral. Emperán was summoned to the council chamber on a plea of very serious business. There he met with the demand that he would be good enough to accept the presidency of a Junta at Caracas. Spain being no longer in a condition to deal with the affairs of the New World, the country could govern itself. Before the urgency of the patriots, Emperán was obliged to give way. He signed several acts. The crowd, egged on by confederates who were distributed here and there among them, prevented him from speaking when he appeared upon the balcony. When he went out the guard did not even present arms, their captain being in the plot. In desperation Emperán resigned his offices; he was paid a good sum in compensation and escorted to La Guayra, where he was obliged to embark in the next boat that sailed for Spain.

The Junta of Caracas called itself at first the Junta to preserve the rights of Ferdinand VII. They did not at that time dream of proclaiming the fall of the monarchy; they simply wished to administer the country themselves. They had a manifesto sent to all the *cabildas* to this effect:

'All those in whom too long a servitude has not killed every hope of redress should follow the patriots of Caracas. Thus they will gain the esteem of those nations who can appreciate enlightened patriotism. You all are called upon to spread these ideas among the people whose leaders you are, rekindle their enthusiasm in the name of the great union of Spanish America.'

At the time of this *coup d'état*, Bolivar was still in the country. He received the news as he was finishing dinner. Leaping onto his horse, Simon avoided the great thickets of thorny creepers, skirted the vast swamps where wading birds stared at him unmoved, where lizards fled at the sound of his horse's hoofs, and where coral snakes, *voladores*, and rattlesnakes made off into the long grass. Bolivar paid no heed to any of them. He knew the road by heart. What was he to believe? Sometimes he exaggerated the victory, sometimes he feared that he had been deceived. He was impatient to be there, and spurred his horse to the utmost.

Without taking breath, Bolivar rushed to Bello's house, where he heard everything.

Bolivar went to the Council of the Junta and informed them of his military rank, for which purpose he had brought the papers with him:

Name: D. Simon Bolivar.

Born at: Caracas.

Date: July 12th, 1783.

Family: noble.

Health: good.

Entered the service: January 14th, 1797.

Campaigns and engagements: none.

Rank: captain (has served in the militia).

Courage: proved.

Diligence: proved.

Ability: proved.

Conduct: proved.

State: widower.

There followed several signatures and seals.

The Junta appointed Bolivar lieutenant-colonel in the militia. At this moment he enters history.

VIII

LIBERAL ideas were making astonishing progress in all the Spanish colonies. At Buenos Ayres and at Santiago de Chile the cause of independence seemed to be won. At Santa Fé an argument in a draper's shop degenerated into a riot. The confederates ran through the town shouting, 'They are murdering the Americans! Long live the Junta!' The patriots called themselves 'representatives of the nation,' a name which had an excellent effect upon the masses. There were acts of heroism. When the garrison seemed about to fire, a woman put herself at the head of the demonstrators and said to her five-year-old son: 'Go and die like a man. We women will march ahead, and if the cannon mow us down, we shall at least have saved the lives of those behind us, who can seize the guns.' The child began to cry, the soldiers fraternized with the insurgents, and the Viceroy realized that resistance was impossible.

At Caracas all was joy; the people believed that they were actually free. Spain was a long way off; rejoicings were organized everywhere. The Junta decided to send ambassadors to London to demand British recognition of the accomplished fact. But whom were they to send? The expenses were enormous and the Junta had not a farthing.

Bolivar offered to bear all the cost himself; he had been in England before, had friends there. He was

accepted. He took with him Luis Lopez Mendez and
Bello, the perennial secretary. Admiral Cochrane put
at their disposal the General Lord Wellington, which
happened at that moment to be returning from Bar-
bados to Great Britain.

Bolivar departed full of hope. He was trusted, he
was accustomed to travelling and to society, knew
several languages, was elegant, and a good speaker.
He was promoted to the rank of colonel and given the
title of 'Chief Representative of Caracas.' Venezuela
felt itself already a great nation.

During the passage Bolivar and his companions re-
hearsed their speeches, questions, and answers. They
had been given long detailed instructions, calculated
not to alienate King George III and to prove the justice of their claims.

They landed at Southampton, stayed there for only
a few hours, and came to London, where rooms had
been reserved for them at Morin's Hotel. The first
interview was fixed for July 17th.

England wished to intimidate Spain by giving a
favourable reception to the envoys of her rebel colonies; to refuse all aid to Venezuela on the pretext of an
allegiance with Spain; and to propose herself for the
rôle of mediator, by which she would gain the gratitude of both parties, without having declared herself
for either.

Bolivar brought credentials purporting to come
from Ferdinand VII, but, in the presence of the Eng-

lish statesmen, driven by a passion beyond his con-
trol, he spoke no longer in the name of the King of
Spain and the Indies, but entirely in the cause of independence for a country unjustly oppressed, which
burned to rid itself of a hateful yoke.

Lord Wellington gave him to understand that England could do nothing for such an object and that a
strict alliance with the Council of Regency at Seville
forbade him to interfere in an affair that was purely
Spanish. All that he could promise was to protect the
New World against a French attack, presuming that
Joseph Bonaparte remained King of the Peninsula.

Bolivar attempted to console himself for this rebuff.
Dressed with the utmost elegance, he walked in
Hyde Park; people turned round to look at him; they
called him the South American ambassador. He was
invited to important balls, he went to the Opera,
where he was the focus of all eyes; the Earl of Morn-
ington and the Duke of Gloucester came every day to
visit him; he went to the races, staked and won. He
was introduced to Gill, the fashionable painter, who
did his portrait in a colonel's full-dress uniform with a
tricolour ribbon round his neck, holding a medal on
which was engraved: 'No Country without Freedom.'

All the youth of London used to meet in Gill's
studio in Chandler Street. While Bolivar posed, fenc-
ing and music went on. The boxers John Gully and
Gregson gave exhibitions with their bare fists. Lord
Byron, back from Turkey, related his exploits as a

swimmer. Bolivar took some lessons in sword-play with a celebrated master-at-arms, who congratulated him upon his aptitude.

The papers were unanimous in praising the charm and elegance of the Venezuelans. Bolivar was happy. He studied the British Constitution and dreamed of introducing it into his own country, but with some modifications, for he had read Montesquieu.

On July 31st, the Council of Regency at Seville declared the Tierra Firme to be in a state of blockade on account of open rebellion. (Tierra Firme was the name for all the north of Spanish America.) England was still an ally of Spain; Bolivar's errand was now pointless. He remained, however, in London, whose attractions he could not bring himself to leave. He met Miranda, who had just sent a letter of congratulation to the Junta of Caracas.

Miranda was still in full career and had given up none of his projects. The Spanish secret police were at his heels; it was known that the American Viceroy had put a price of thirty thousand dollars on his head.

'Not enough to pay my debts,' as he himself declared.

Bolivar, having no longer any official mission, was delighted to meet Miranda openly. The two men became inseparable. Miranda lived in Grafton Square, Piccadilly. All the political refugees in England used to meet at his house.

The 'Morning Chronicle' and the 'Edinburgh Review' published impassioned articles, appeals to

George III, magnificent plans for a pan-American confederation. The Government informed Bolivar that they had armed the brig Sapphire especially for him and that he must not defer his departure. Bolivar parted with tears from Miranda, who entrusted him with all his baggage and swore to rejoin him as soon as possible. Two hundred people put themselves to the trouble of accompanying Bolivar as far as the quay at Portsmouth.

The boat sailed on the 21st of September. Handkerchiefs were waved. Bolivar was anxious to regain Caracas, where the blockade must already have begun. He had with him two Indian slaves, José and Juan Pablo. Bolivar set them free. The slaves thanked him without understanding it, and Captain Davies, though an old hand, could not get over this fine bit of posturing.

The British flag was a guarantee of safety. Moreover, no Spanish ship showed itself on the horizon.

Shoals of sharks followed the Sapphire for miles, and leaning over the bulwarks Bolivar flung to them all the records of his embassy, which he no longer knew how to dispose of.

IX

THREE men were at the head of affairs at Caracas:
Juan Escalona, Cristobal Mendoza, and Baltasar
Padrón. Such confusion had never before been seen.

After several weeks of rejoicings it was seen that
the situation was beginning to grow complicated.
Several towns had recognized the Regency. At Lima
the Spanish garrison had sacked the rich part of the
town and on a feeble excuse had massacred hundreds
of people. Puerto Cabello had become a centre of
counter-revolution. Talk of punishing the rebels was
beginning everywhere.

The Junta decided to send the Marquis del Toro
with four thousand men against the town of Cora.
The Marquis possessed four field-guns, but no ammunition. His men were armed with knives, with iron
bars, clubs, and old swords; a hundred or so had muskets. It was deplorable. At the Spaniards' first dis-
charge, there was a wholesale stampede.

Bolivar's brother had been sent to the United
States to buy arms. An unscrupulous dealer persuaded him, instead of arms, to take agricultural im-
plements, which would certainly be of more service
to the prosperity of Venezuela. Nobody understood
the working of his machines, the need for which was
nowhere apparent. Moreover, the ship which brought
them foundered in a storm and Juan Vicente only escaped death by a miracle.

Bolivar was furious, and, no sooner returned, withdrew to one of his country estates.

The Junta realized the necessity for immediate action, but what was to be done? Miranda's arrival was announced. To welcome him was quite plainly to declare war with Spain. What of it? In the pass to which they had come, what matter a little more or a little less? A resolute man was needed and Miranda appeared as a saviour. They prepared to receive him with pomp. The delegates who were to meet him had studied a little address: 'Your country will appear to you greatly changed. The former tyranny has made way for a government which thinks only of the well-being of the nation, a sentiment which has always been your pride.'

When Miranda's ship was sighted, they fired a salute. A boat put off for the shore. Miranda was seated in the stern, bareheaded, holding the tiller while four men kept time with their oars.

The delegates were dressed in incredible costumes, braided to the armholes, with pistols in their belts, swords trailing, and spurs as big as open hands.

Miranda observed them pityingly.

Simon Bolivar arrived on horseback dressed in better taste, a dark blue suit, grey cravat, the famous high-crowned hat with a flat brim turned up at the sides, but down at the front and back.

Miranda inquired of him where was the army which he, a general of France, could command without losing his prestige.

The crowd acclaimed the Forerunner with modera-
tion. They were not much reassured by the sight of
this surly-looking giant who had knocked about all
over the world and made so much talk with his regi-
cide ideas and his adventures.

A meal had been prepared at Bolivar's house.
While he was eating, Miranda felt himself full of
bitterness and grief. He had expected to find an organized and enthusiastic state, with brave and well-
armed soldiers. He found Caracas dirtier than ever,
barefoot men none of whom knew their drill, and it
was from this that he was to make a republic. He
thought of Frederick the Great's guards on parade,
of Potemkin's cavalry, of the magnificent regiments
of Sambre-et-Meuse. Here there were only hang-
dog ragamuffins.

These people deserved the Spanish yoke, and talked
of independence. What a delusion!

Bolivar tried to make him understand that the
situation was not so bad, that all these lads were
brave, that with a little patience they would make
wonderful soldiers.

'What do you know about it?' demanded Miranda.

'I am a colonel of militia.'

'Then that finishes it! A colonel! A colonel! Look
here, this is not the time to joke. Have you ever
heard of Turenne, Condé, Marshal Saxe? Do you
know how to draw up a plan of battle? You think
that the only thing is to fall on the enemy; you are a
child. You will start as second lieutenant. Even that

is a great deal; we shall see what you are fit for. And this imbecile Marquis del Toro, who has appointed himself general and can scarcely stand upright. Ah, you have sent for me; you shall see that I am not here for my own amusement. To work, and quickly. Believe me there is going to be a change.'

And there was.

In view of the alarming news that arrived, Miranda established a committee of public safety. He set up camps where the recruits learned to march as did Napoleon's soldiers and to execute combined manœuvres. They were taught the movements for firing, sword-play, and bayonet exercise. Miranda bawled.

He wrote to France for instructor officers to be sent out. Not an instant's respite did he give himself. All day at the parade ground, he broke his fast on his feet and with his hat on. He jeered at the beautiful theory which holds that in time of danger the populace will rise of itself and repel the invaders. One does not fight with moral ideas and Utopias; one fights with regular troops who are trained to arms.

Arsenals were built and munitions manufactured. In the evenings Miranda returned to Caracas, attended all the meetings and made fiery speeches. The people listened and obeyed him.

However, a Spanish officer who had offered his services to the Junta and who had been entrusted with an important post, disappeared with all the plans for mobilization.

This time there could be no more delay.

X

IT was no longer a moment for disputing details or delaying over paltry quarrels. People realized the serious state of affairs and at all the public meetings they showed an unaccustomed zeal. They no longer defended the rights of Ferdinand VII against Bonaparte or the Regency; they spoke of a republic, and the rights which they asserted were the rights of man.

All the representatives of the public assembled on July 3 [1811], in the cathedral. No other roofed place was so large. A tribune had been arranged in front of the altar, an immense table set up and covered with a red cloth.

At ten in the morning, Miranda arrived, delegate for the obscure commune of Pao. He strode up and down examining the fifteenth-century Stations of the Cross. Bolivar was all on edge. He felt that something extraordinary was going to happen.

When the deputies were all there, the main doors were opened and the crowd was allowed to enter, held back by barriers of prayer desks.

President Rodriguez Domingues opened the session on the question of absolute independence. Immediately there was an uproar; it was who could speak first. There were noblemen, young and old, priests, officers, merchants; the speeches followed one another all day in an atmosphere of passion. The heat was stifling; the orators were not exhausted, but the session was declared closed. It seemed that the people were not yet ripe, nor the deputies either. They were watching for a favourable minute when the vote would be unanimous, and hoped for a chance upon the next day.

The cathedral emptied itself; the doors remained open and the nave in confusion. In the square the argument went on for hours. People stayed up all night.

On the 4th of July, anniversary of the freedom of the United States, the debate was resumed more fiercely than ever.

On the 5th, feeling the audience to be in a paroxysm of enthusiasm, Miranda announced that Masséna had just been defeated in Spain; that a treaty with France would be the fatal consequence of this victory of Seville, which would then without delay turn its mind to an expedition against Venezuela.

Every one sprang up with cries of 'Long live the Republic!' and 'Down with slavery!' They demanded total independence. In a moment of intoxication the 'Declaration of Independence of Venezuela,' drawn up by Roscio and Isnardy, was signed by the forty-one deputies.

It was announced at once to the crowd, horsemen went off in every direction to spread the news. All night long bonfires burned in the streets and men embraced one another. The only talk was of crushing the Spaniards should they dare to show themselves.

In the taverns various persons, considered by the drunkards to be too lukewarm, narrowly escaped murder, and people drew their knives ready to stab the Castilians.

A Spanish squadron on its way from Porto Rico tried to disembark at Cumaná, but a quickly organized resistance prevented them from landing. This little victory raised men's spirits; they believed themselves to be already out of danger.

The colours proposed by Miranda for the national flag were adopted. In the square, where eleven years earlier the Spaniards had beheaded his father, España's son presented to the army a standard of yellow, blue, and red.

On the 14th of July, anniversary of the French Revolution, there were illuminations and fireworks, and in all the houses people danced.

The statues of Ferdinand VII and Charles IV were broken up.

XI

AFTER some exceedingly deadly street fighting in
which Bolivar behaved with admirable courage,
Miranda took Valencia and restored Bolivar to his
rank of colonel. Valencia was a place where reaction
was especially to be feared. Unfortunately for himself, Miranda could not take advantage of his success;
he was recalled to Caracas, where the jealousy and
hatred of the Creole aristocracy were doing their best
to have him condemned for lack of firmness towards
the Spaniards. Every one fancied himself a Robespierre. Miranda treated the accusations with contempt; he disbanded his army.

The Spaniards resumed the offensive everywhere.
Victories and defeats and again victories, never a de-
cisive battle.

The Spanish general Monteverde entered Siqui-
sique, massacred the inhabitants, and, raising the
whole rural population for the King's cause, marched
upon Barquisemeto.

The rebels awaited him with courage; they wished
to finish the matter once and for all, but a frightful
catastrophe befell to shatter their hopes.

At Caracas on the 26th of March, a beautiful day
in Holy Week, processions followed the clergy and
choir-boys to the cathedral. People felt confident
of the future. The independent flag floated from every building. They were happy; they talked about

Monteverde's advance, but without misgiving; the enemy would be driven back; the men who had been sent against them were the most seasoned soldiers in the garrison. It was two years since Venezuela had felt her power, and had expelled the Captain-General. Since then no threat had made the patriots flinch.

In the middle of the afternoon the sky grew suddenly dark, a peal of thunder broke with a terrific crash. The earth began to quake. Houses crumbled, the streets split into deep crevasses, terrified horses bolted, people fled like madmen, children screamed, whole families disappeared into gulfs which opened in a single instant. Fires broke out on every side, cabins were reduced to ashes.

The procession was taken by surprise; tapers, stoles, banners, still-smoking censers lay abandoned on the ground. Mothers called for their children, husbands for their wives. There was panic, for the earth had not stopped trembling and shock succeeded shock. People did not know where to take refuge. To avoid the stones and falling beams, they congregated in the centre of the square; the place suddenly sank in, and they were swallowed up. The thousands of bodies with heads crushed were horrible to see. The injured screamed terribly, but no one came to their help. An aged man was dragging himself away, both legs in tatters; a balcony fell on him.

Thieves tried to take advantage of the confusion; they made their way into the rich houses whose doors had been torn off. They were seen to come out again laden with booty, but their careers were not long, for they in their turn disappeared beneath the ruins.

Bolivar and some of his friends went through the town carrying stretchers. The earth had ceased to quake; there were almost ten thousand people missing in Caracas alone. Even those who had come through bore the marks of the disaster, and every one that appeared was limping or had a bandaged head or his arm in a sling.

The people did not know which way to turn; they were afraid of the few houses that still stood and did not dare to go into them for fear of a fresh shock. In the ravaged streets, upon heaps of stones or ashes, beside unrecognizable corpses, the inhabitants of Caracas remained curdled with terror. Bolivar with magnificent energy went from one group to another, collected the wounded, and organized an open-air hospital. His own house was nothing but ruins, his books, his furniture, his clothes scattered all about. He did not give them a thought.

The towns of Merida, Barquisimeto, and San Felipe were destroyed. At La Guayra only one house remained standing, that of an Englishman who was away travelling at the time. The troops who had been sent against Monteverde were annihilated. The stores of munitions, the magazines, and the gun parks had not been spared.

By a freakish chance no towns had escaped the disaster except those that had remained faithful to the Spaniards. Monteverde had not lost a man. Before their ruined churches the priests in many places preached a return to the old régime, in order to recover their influence, undermined by the revolution.

'God has wished to punish the patriots and the dissolute morals of the Venezuelans. The anniversary of d'Emperán's banishment had been chosen by God for the execution of His justice. Two years, and the chastisement has proved terrible.'

The people, always fanatical, were stirred; couples who had lived together without being married had their union blessed without delay. Every one felt guilty of something and recalled to mind Scriptural memories of Sodom and Gomorrah. Such was their fear for themselves that they hardly thought of mourning for the dead. The position was absolutely lost; the Spaniards might come, nobody could make any further resistance.

Bolivar found in his path a priest, engaged in exhorting the people to submit themselves to the King; he drew his sword, scattered the audience, drove away the orator, and, standing upon a heap of rubbish, brandishing his weapon, he shouted:

'Ah, Nature is in league with despotism. She hopes to stop us. The worse for her, we shall know how to force her to obey.'

Those who heard him were impressed, but Caracas was in ruins.

XII

THE towns were rebuilding everywhere.

Miranda had appointed himself Dictator and Generalissimo of the land and sea forces of Venezuela. He returned to Caracas to call to arms every Venezuelan, whatever his rank in life or his colour. Slaves were to be restored to freedom as the price of ten years' military service. Recruits were taken by force, and men were brought in with handcuffs on their wrists; they were immediately drafted into barracks, where they were trained before they knew it. They often made excellent soldiers. They did not have very regular meals, they were paid in paper money and their outfit was not very uniform; but what did it matter? Men were needed.

With this army of rookies Miranda beat the Spaniards twice, and Monteverde had the greatest difficulty in escaping.

Miranda gave a dinner of a hundred covers to his officers.

His general staff was almost entirely composed of foreigners, Irish, Scotch, and above all, French.

While they were eating, the officers related their adventures: 'Before I came here to command the Venezuelan cavalry,' declared Serviez, 'I went through some bad times. I was a captain of dragoons under Napoleon and everybody spoke of the brilliant future in store for me. One day at a ball I made the acquaintance of a general's wife. I do not know how it happened, but I became her lover. When I was wounded in Spain, my mistress forgot all caution and left her husband to come and nurse me. The scandal obliged us both to fly to England. We were not married and it was difficult for us to get work. We were just beginning to find employment when the birth of a child plunged us back into poverty. We sailed for the United States, where I hoped to enter the army. They had no use for me; and as the months passed we became more and more destitute. Then it was that I heard of the revolution in Tierra Firme, and the arrival of Miranda. I came here without delay. My mistress has stayed at Boston with a relation who was willing to be responsible for her and for our child, but who will not hear of me.'

'I am Scotch,' said MacGregor, 'and I have never liked England. I deserted because I did not choose to fight against France. I shipped as a common sailor on board a Dutch privateer. I became second in command, and one day, after a dispute, I fought with my captain and killed him. Promoted to be commander of the pirate ship, I voyaged all over Oceania. I seized an island not very far from Florida, and there I founded a sort of headquarters for all the freebooters in the West Indies. They came to me to repair their ships, and to buy arms and munitions. I wearied of this too easy existence. Miranda sounded to me like a congenial leader and I offered him my sword. When the war is over, I shall perhaps go back to my trade of pirate; later I shall retire to a Pacific island which I know of and I shall have myself made a king by the natives, who are friends of mine.'

'We will give our blood if it is needed for the liberty of Venezuela. What Lafayette and Rochambeau did for Washington, we will do for Miranda!' cried Châtillon, du Cayla, and Schombourg, all three former captains of Hussar regiments.

There was brawn and bravery to spare.

Miranda had the most profound contempt for the Creoles. The only one who found any favour with him was Lieutenant Soublette, because he was of Franche-Comté stock.

They spoke only French.

For once in a way Miranda had done things well; not the highly spiced cookery to which he could not accustom himself, but dishes prepared as they were in Paris. There were real wines and real liqueurs to drink; a centrepiece in the Venezuelan colours was in the middle of the table. Indians brought in new dishes in ceaseless succession. Fans waved in the immense barn where the meal was served. While Miranda gave advice to Pedro Gual, who was going as ambassador to the United States, and sketched for him the principal people that he would meet, the French officers revived memories of European wars. Cigars were lit and coffee served.

Colonel Bussy entered the room, and, bending over

the General, whispered into his ear. Miranda rose
and made his excuses — an urgent message, he would
return at once.

In the porch a dusty messenger handed him a letter; Miranda opened it and read:

General, an officer unworthy to be called Venezuelan has seized the fort of San Felipe with the as-
sistance of the prisoners who were confined there, and
is now engaged in a terrible bombardment of the
town. If Your Excellency does not immediately
attack the enemy in the rear, Puerto Cabello is lost.
Till then I shall defend the place by every possible
means.

SIMON BOLIVAR

Miranda sank onto a bench. The banquet was nothing to him. Venezuela had just been wounded to
the heart.

XIII

PUERTO CABELLO was so called because a single hair would suffice to moor a ship there in the Gulf of Triste, marvellously sheltered for such a mountainous coast. Long sandy beaches stretched beneath hills covered with giant cactus. The town was much prettier than La Guayra; the streets were wider, the houses better kept. There was a public garden in the midst of charming walks. Nothing was to be heard but the sound of a stream which ran down towards the sea, and whose noise in the end passed unnoticed, like the ticking of a clock.

Bolivar was not there for pleasure. The place was important and would command any future landings. The rank of garrison commandant has few thrills for an ardent young officer who is only happy when he is leading his troops to the attack. No matter, he was obliged to make up his mind to it. Miranda did not like Bolivar's way of conducting himself; he had made cutting remarks after a review because the latter had caracoled at the head of his division. Miranda was mixing the Old and the New Worlds. All the same you could not put shakos or plumed helmets onto the Venezuelans. The best stimulant for them was to show one's self fearless; to raise their enthusiasm, to lead them to battle as if it were a bull-fight.

Bolivar was bored. He had had a floor made upon a piece of level ground and practised sword-play with his friends. But one cannot fence all day long. Ignacio played the guitar and sang, but he knew only six songs. And to ride in the park, where he knew every blade of grass —— The only amusement was to make his organization the strictest possible.

The citadel commanded the town and forbade any attack from outside. The guns were mounted, heaps of bullets prepared; four hundred hundredweight of powder, lead, and three hundred carefully placed guns.

All the Spanish prisoners were confined in the jail, guarded night and day by Francesco Vinoni and Captain Carbonell. There was no means of escape. Bolivar had every confidence in Carbonell, who had covered himself with glory in various engagements.

The news on the whole was good. Monteverde was reorganizing his army, but after two reverses he needed a breathing space before resuming the offensive.

Bolivar lived in a room at the Town Hall. It was not very comfortable, but he was freer there than in a private house. He went in and out unconcerned as to time and with no fear of disturbing any one. He had only a mattress, a basin, and two chairs; his table had lost one leg, but he pushed it up against a wall and it stood there.

On the 30th of June, he had left the citadel a little earlier than usual; he had an appointment with a commandant to draw up a plan of concerted action between the divisions in the field. The two men dis-

cussed the arrangement over their wine; they went on
talking till it was fairly late and took a stroll before
they went to bed. Bolivar was slow in falling asleep;
he thought for a long time that night about a possible
exchange of duty with a comrade. There were many
who would ask nothing better than to take his place.

It was almost eleven in the morning when he woke.
Through the open window the sea showed calm as
ever. He dressed himself at leisure.

Towards noon an explosion was heard, followed by
several others. A shot fell in the public gardens; a
little girl was knocked over.

No ship in sight — mysterious.

Bolivar looked at the citadel, saw smoke, a whole
troop upon the ramparts, guns belching over the
town. There was no doubt of it, the bombardment
came from the fort; with a glass one could distinguish
Carbonell and Vinoni directing the fire, and the
Spanish prisoners, now free, carrying out their orders.

There had been treachery.

At Puerto Cabello there remained only the cavalry,
quartered in the great red barracks. There was no
artillery, little ammunition. There were only rations
for a day or two. It was impossible to fight. What
was to be done?

Bolivar had an entrenchment dug, and earthworks
were thrown up rapidly, for the barracks made a too
easy target. A man went off with the famous letter
to Miranda. The port must be defended no matter
how. The citadel was impregnable; an attack would

be madness. They must hold on as long as possible. Since they could not return the fire, they must keep quiet, hide, sham dead. Perhaps the traitors would decide to come down; in the streets one might have tried one's luck.

They collected together all the provisions; there were even less than they had thought. They divided them so as to last as long as possible. Water was scarce, and the heat so overpowering that at the end of a few hours the men were quarrelling over the water-skins. How could they hold out under such conditions?

An excited movement was observed among the people in the citadel; what was happening? Bolivar went up onto the church tower, from which he could see to an immense distance. On the road, a few kilometres away, were troops upon the march. Was it Miranda? His heart leapt wildly. Alas! he had to change his tune. The Spanish flag was at the head of these troops. He was to be attacked from every side at once. There was no time to hesitate. Should he risk a sortie? Miles and Jalon went out with two hundred horse to repel the advance guard. At the first encounter the men went over to the enemy, and Miles returned with but seven of them.

Bolivar realized that all was lost. The taking of Puerto Cabello by the enemy was serious, but he could not with the paltry detachment who remained faithful to him successfully repulse five or six thousand Spaniards, and on the other side withstand continuous shell fire. Puerto Cabello could not be held. The point was how to avoid falling into the hands of Monteverde. They must take advantage of the darkness to make their escape.

That evening after sunset the horizon turned purple. The night fell suddenly, there was a storm in the air. By good luck the darkness was so thick that in a few minutes the palm trees on the promenade were invisible at five yards' distance. Bolivar with five officers and three men made their way towards a little clump of mangroves upon a neck of land in which a small boat was hidden. It was a modest fishing smack drawn up onto the beach; they launched it, and took to the oars, for the sail might have been noticed. They had to get away quickly, but without a sound. Puerto Cabello seemed asleep. A few lights showed in the citadel. Bolivar took the tiller, compass in hand, the others rowed, gently, because the splashing of the water sounded loud in such a silence. They had to leave the coast without being seen by the Spanish ships, which were certainly cruising not far away. It was at least forty leagues to La Guayra. When Bolivar considered that they were sufficiently clear, he had the sail hoisted. A light breeze luckily was blowing, they were beginning to grow tired at the oars. A lamp put into the crown of an upside-down hat allowed them to follow the course upon a chart. They spoke but few words, and in a whisper. The darkness was so deep that they almost groped their way. Not a star was in the sky.

Miles, overcome with sleep, had stretched himself on the deck. Bolivar thought of poor Jalon, deserted by his men, whom the Spaniards had taken prisoner. Was he even alive now?

When the sun rose, the boat was in the open sea. It was raining, but no one thought of complaining. They had to reach La Guayra at all costs, and fatigue was only an incident, the least important one in this adventure.

XIV

In circumstances more than difficult, Miranda was making superhuman efforts.

In the mines at Barquisimeto the Spaniards had regained very important material of war which they had considered lost for ever. The negroes rebelled, burned the country houses, and murdered their masters. Miranda protected the towns from pillage and crushed the negro rising, but he felt clearly that the end was coming.

He summoned a Council at Victoria to consider what steps to take; there were present: F. Espejo, J. G. Roscio, Casa-León, F. A. Paul, and Sata y Bussy. All were of opinion that they must treat with Monteverde. The Spaniards occupied three quarters of the country, and threatened Caracas. But Miranda knew very well that their terms would be ruinous. He needed a victory even if it were a short-lived one; a success would allow him to be more exacting; he must make them think that he had still some resources.

On July 11th he attacked the enemy.

On the 12th, Monteverde granted an armistice to discuss the terms. Sata y Bussy and Manuel Aldoa came to his headquarters at Valencia. Miranda as Dictator demanded the evacuation of certain villages, recognition of the Venezuelan Constitution, and liberty for those who wished to leave the country. No one was to be victimized for revolutionary actions or opinions. There was to be a complete amnesty for all parties.

Monteverde agreed to the demand for an amnesty, but insisted on the surrender of all fortified places.

Miranda's envoys were so impressed and were so desirous to curry favour with the Spanish general that at San Mateo they signed everything that he put before them. They even went so far as to give Monteverde permission to apply the surrender clauses personally.

All those who had insisted upon the Dictator concluding peace took their turn now to reproach him for what they called ignoble cowardice. Miranda had no further influence with any one; his own soldiers would obey him no longer; they turned away without saluting. They accused him of treason. 'When a man has still five thousand men, when he has dragged a country into a disastrous war, he should go on to the end and not thus abandon his native land.' They recalled all their grievances and Miranda's contempt for the Creoles. Now that the lion was no longer dangerous, they avenged themselves on him by words.

As he entered Caracas an officer flung himself upon Miranda and tried to stab him. Miranda avoided the blade, felled his assailant with a blow upon the jaw, and turned towards his escort, not one of whom had stirred. With clenched teeth and quivering with fury, he himself had his assailant locked up. Then he re-

tired to his house and did not leave it for the rest of
the day.

Next day he went to La Guayra to superintend the
departure of the patriots. He forbade any foreign
vessels to leave the port. An English captain came
and besought him to lift the embargo; his ship, which
was no other than the Sapphire, was laden with mer-
chandise of great value and a very considerable sum
of money. Miranda consented to take the money
into his charge, but refused to escape upon the boat,
as the captain had offered if the embargo were lifted.

Miranda had had a little room prepared for him in
the house of Casas, who was governor of the town.
He lay down fully dressed upon a sofa and ordered
his aide-de-camp Soublette to wake him at sunrise.

The room was upstairs.

Down below in the dining-room, Casas was con-
spiring against his benefactor. He had realized that
Miranda could be of no further use to him. The thing
now was to make favour with the Spaniards:

'The Dictator is nothing more nor less than a
traitor to his country. Has he not accepted a large
sum of money from the captain of the Sapphire to
allow that vessel to leave the port? The Englishman
was here again just now, which shows that the two
men are in collusion.'

'Miranda,' said some one else, 'has even sent his
baggage to the Sapphire's launch. I saw it with my
own eyes. He is going to desert us at sunrise.'

In this ill-lit dining-room the argument grew bitter. Even Bolivar, who had just arrived, was perturbed by it. Appearances were against the Generalissimo. Moreover, he had not come to the rescue of Puerto Cabello. While Bolivar was making a desperate resistance, when he was forced to flee in the middle of the night, the Dictator was negotiating with Monteverde in spite of his still intact army.

An officer rose.

'The Spaniards are coming. They will do what they choose with this town and with ourselves, but before that Miranda shall face a court-martial and answer for his treason.'

Men were posted in the street to prevent the Dictator from escaping through a window. Casas, de Peña, Bolivar, and several others went up to the first floor. They ordered Soublette to rouse the Generalissimo. Soublette knocked at the door. A sleepy voice answered:

'Already? Come, come! It is much too soon. Let me have another hour or two of sleep.'

But all the same Miranda could be heard moving about his room. He opened the door and appeared on the threshold.

'What is happening? Have the Spaniards come already?'

Bolivar addressed him. 'General, we must ask you to be good enough to consider yourself our prisoner, and to give us an explanation of your conduct.'

Miranda took a lighted candle out of Soublette's

hand, and holding it on a level with their faces recited the names of those who had just arrested him.

'Fools! Will you never be able to do anything except make a noise?'

He unhooked his sword and flung it down the stairs.

'After you, gentlemen.'

He was taken to the port of San Carlos. On the way there he opened his mouth only once, to demand a cigar. He halted for an instant to light it and resumed his way without a word.

At seven o'clock in the morning an order arrived from Monteverde to prohibit the departure of any ships whatever. There was no more question of a treaty. Terror reigned in La Guayra, haphazard shooting, pillage, and massacre; the streets were red with blood.

Hidden by a miracle in an Indian's house, Bolivar did not stir out for several days.

Miranda was removed by the Spaniards to the underground dungeons of Puerto Cabello before being sent to the prison at Cadiz, where in 1816 he died of grief. He confided these words to a companion of his captivity:

'My friend, the Spanish fetters seem to me less heavy than those which I had to wear in my native land.'

XV

LISTS of suspects were drawn up every day. The regular executioners no longer sufficed. Such atrocities were committed that the Spaniards in Monteverde's suite themselves were sickened; but rebels were being punished and it was necessary to disgust a whole nation with revolution, once and for all.

Bolivar took refuge in Caracas, in the house of a very important personage, the Marquis of Casa-León; there he met once more a Spanish officer called Don Francisco Iturbe, whom he had known well in Madrid and who had influence with the Commander-in-Chief. Iturbe offered him a passport. The part that Bolivar had played in Miranda's arrest might serve as an excuse, and Monteverde would have been glad to make it known publicly that the most prominent gentleman in Venezuela had helped in the pacification of the country. Bolivar refused to lend himself to this deception. If he had arrested Miranda, it was solely because he had believed him to be a traitor to his country and in the pay of the King of Spain. Iturbe let him talk, treated him as incorrigible, and procured him a safe-conduct to Curaçao.

Bolivar embarked with José Felix Rivas on a Spanish schooner which was to put in at that island. He was ashamed of it, but he did not relinquish his opinions; this was perhaps only the means to an end. So much the better.

He arrived at Curaçao, but the schooner's papers were not in order and the local authorities took possession of the whole contents of the ship, including Bolivar's luggage.

This time Bolivar had not a halfpenny.

He had succeeded in saving a fair amount of ready money. He brought a lawsuit, but the legal business was desperately slow, and Bolivar was obliged to live on the pickings of some Venezuelan refugees more provident than himself.

The island was not populous; after having been Dutch it had become English.

Bolivar, whose history was known, was well enough received, but his money was not returned to him. Every day he walked in the sugar-cane plantations, beneath orange trees and palms like those of his own country. He fed on the fruit which he picked on the way — guavas, alligator pears, chirimoyas, mangoes, and cinnamons. Rivas accompanied him, no richer than himself. The same subject gave heat to their conversation, fury at being there helpless among those flowers, those asclepias, while Venezuela was being crushed by the enemy.

Bolivar wrote to Iturbe to thank him, and also to ask for news of the situation. Iturbe replied with an announcement that all the Bolivar family estates had been confiscated. This was utter ruin.

Every evening the Venezuelan patriots, feeling

DOOR OF THE BOLIVAR HOUSE

themselves absolute aliens on this island, used to meet at a little wine-shop, more to exchange talk than to drink.

The Spaniards had taken possession of all Venezuela, but the mountains still debarred them from New Granada, whose civil wars seemed to have died down and where the flag of independence still floated. Without any doubt Monteverde would organize an expedition against these Liberals; the outbreak of war could not be long delayed.

Bolivar made up his mind. He sold his last jewels, even the medal which he had worn in London when he posed in Gill's studio. He took his passage on an English brig which was sailing for Cartagena.

XVI

At Cartagena of the Indies, the port for New Granada, Bolivar interviewed President Torres. The fame of his courage had passed the Cordilleras. Bolivar was authorized to serve with his rank of colonel; he was commended to General Labatut, who ordered him forthwith to occupy the advanced post at Barraca on the Magdalena River.

Before Bolivar parted from his friends, he left with them the manuscript of a declaration which he had written during his passage; he asked them to be good enough to have it printed and to distribute copies here and there about the country. This was promised, and Bolivar started up the Magdalena on a raft.

On the 15th of December, a fortnight after his departure, the proclamation appeared, under the title of 'The Manifesto of the Venezuelan Colonel Simon Bolivar to the people of New Granada.'

The manifesto was fairly long, and contained the following statements:

'If Venezuela has given way, the chief blame lies with her leaders, who sought their inspiration in books written by visionaries. They tried to found a perfect political system on the basis of the perfection of the human race. We have been led by philosophers, our laws made by philanthropists, our tactics decided by dialecticians and our army commanded by sophists. . . .

'Our military organization was deplorable. No one would hear of a regular army. We had nothing but an ignorant and undisciplined militia which cost us more than regular mercenaries. The national wealth went in useless and shameful expenses; a crowd of officials without definite employment have ruined the country, and we have been obliged to have recourse to the miserable system of paper money.

'Our ruin was completed by the establishment of the federal government, entirely contrary to our interests. The earthquake of March 26th undoubtedly staggered the country physically and morally, but it gave it an opportunity to realize the lack of energy of the Junta, unable to rise to the occasion, incapable either of organizing relief or of bringing help to the injured. A sacrilegious clergy in the Spanish pay has made unchallenged use of it to influence the people.

'May our experience serve as an example to all the nations of the New World who aspire to independence.

'Our institutions must adapt themselves to the nature of events, circumstances, and human beings. If these are equable, the institutions will be peaceable, but if they are fiery and passionate, the government should be arbitrary and of uncompromising firmness, not allowing itself to be daunted by laws or constitutions.

'Education and military training are indispensable.

'A general cannot be improvised.

'When the nation has been put to the proof and has served her apprenticeship to the Republican virtues, she will be given institutions worthy of her. Meanwhile political theories are not in keeping with our mentality.

'New Granada has seen the rocks upon which Venezuela foundered. There is only one way to escape them. Retake Caracas.

'This scheme will appear at first as a costly, impossible piece of folly, but on examination it will show itself to be no chimera.

'The fall of Venezuela is due to the contempt and indifference in which she has always held the province of Coro, a hotbed of royalist infection whose destruction has been too long delayed. Now, the resources with which Coro was able to supply the Spaniards are as nothing compared to those with which Caracas will supply to them from now on, and which can but increase. There must be no delay. The province of Caracas is a danger which threatens New Granada and may easily be fatal to her.

'The possessions of Granada must first and at once be pacified with whatever rigour is required. As soon as that first task is fulfilled, we will drive the enemy out of the whole of Tierra Firme. Cartagena shall be the keystone of the nation. New Granada owes it to herself to pursue the invaders and to dislodge them from their last strongholds. Venezuela, cradle of Colombian independence, awaits her deliverance.

'Do not close your ears to the prayers of the oppressed, avenge the dead, restore the dying. It is from you alone that the New World hopes for liberty.'

There was a rush for copies of this manifesto and they were posted on every wall.

On his raft, alert to avoid jagged rocks and impenetrable creepers, rousing on his passage jaguars whose eyes glowed through the darkness, followed by the menace of enormous alligators, not even noticing the great poisonous snakes which made off through the reeds, Simon Bolivar felt that a new mission had been entrusted to him; that around him, waiting for him, was a whole nation, which he must organize and set at liberty in spite of its indolence and in spite of a thousand dangers which would have deterred any one but himself.

XVII

GENERAL LABATUT had given Bolivar orders to go to Barranca and there await instructions. The Spaniards held part of the country, and Barranca, on the banks of the Magdalena, was a village of considerable strategic importance.

Bolivar was scarcely there before he reviewed the garrison. There were in all two hundred and fifty men, fairly well equipped. He sent a messenger to President Torres begging to be allowed some initiative. Bolivar undertook to drive back the enemy and establish a stronger line of defence. Torres consented, impressed by so much confidence and decision.

Bolivar took two hundred men, built ten long covered rafts and embarked his soldiers with provisions and gunpowder. The expedition moved off. They advanced upstream, the rafts being pushed by poles on either side. Navigation was fairly easy because the water was at least five feet deep, and there were as yet neither rapids nor sandbanks. Bolivar was at the head of his flotilla; he had forbidden them to shoot at the alligators which slept in groups on the banks. They pushed on without speaking, only the orders passed from one boat to another. It was a matter of speed.

Just before he came in sight of Tenerife, Bolivar anchored his rafts and sent one of his officers to demand the surrender of the Spanish commander.

Then, without even waiting for him to come back, they resumed their progress. The rafts met the officer returning with a refusal. Immediately battle stations were taken up; the armed men in front, while those behind poled vigorously with boat-hooks. The Spanish perceived the sudden onslaught of this strange squadron, which advanced in good order and opened fire. As at this spot the river flows between high banks and forms a complete loop, the Spaniards thought that they had to deal with a large troop, and fled. Bolivar did not lose a man. He found in Tenerife a well-stocked arsenal and shops overflowing with provisions. He stayed there only a few hours and continued his offensive.

He attempted Mompox, a town situated at a four-crossways of water. The Spaniards were driven out and the populace acclaimed the victors. Three hundred recruits came forward and were armed upon the spot.

Bolivar turned his back on the pink periwinkles, and the snake plants which cure the bites of serpents, and whose heart-shaped leaves are used for children's hats. He had reënforced his fleet, and it now consisted of about twenty large boats, of which one or two carried small guns.

He pursued Major Capdevilla, who was beating a retreat towards Chiriguana, overtook and routed him. The same evening he annihilated another enemy detachment at Tamalameque. He took possession of Puerto Real and entered Ocaña, the richest town of that region, where he was received as a saviour.

Starting with two hundred men, Bolivar had in a fortnight beaten three thousand Spaniards and liberated an immense tract of country. His losses were insignificant. The people all declared themselves for Cartagena. The enemies' threat was averted, and communications were reëstablished between the higher and lower Magdalena.

During this time Labatut had taken Santa Marta, and French pirates had sunk a Spanish fleet which was bringing munitions.

Bolivar was obliged to take to his bed; during the whole campaign he had suffered terribly from fever, refusing to take care of himself and getting barely two or three hours' sleep in twenty-four. Until he had fulfilled the mission which he had prescribed for himself, he would take no thought for himself.

XVIII

A SENTRY in front of Bolivar's tent died from the bite of a large blue spider. Fires were lit round the camp to keep off the tigers which prowled about at night.

There was now no question of raging war as Miranda had pictured it: Bolivar was a bandit chief collecting his soldiers no matter where, arming them with muskets captured from the enemy; marching to the attack as soon as the presence of Spaniards was signalled, employing all sorts of ruses, spies, and indirect manœuvres. It was a war of ambush, of surprise attack, and prisoners were only taken that they might be forced to speak. Cowards and the irresolute were executed. The men slept upon the ground without fear of the serpents or the spider-crabs. They ate what they could get. In the middle of the night they would leave their camp, ride through the dark, and fall upon a still sleeping enemy; the slaughter was merciless. Two or three times in a day they would fight, and the bravest won. Every minute brought its heroic deeds.

Young noblemen came to take service with Bolivar: 'If two men are needed to free the country, allow me to be the second.' And all these young people, brought up in refinement, adapted themselves joyfully to the guerrilla life.

The combats were man to man, fists, feet, throttlings, knives; guns went off by themselves. Not a

murmur; privations and fatigue were not enough to
damp their spirits. Bolivar was always at the head;
bullets whistled round him, his horse was killed; pistol
in one hand, sword in the other, nothing daunted him.
The men followed wherever he chose to lead them.
They had confidence in his confidence. He flung himself into such hazardous expeditions and came out of
them with so much honour that it seemed he could do
no wrong.

Feeling himself reëstablished in health, Bolivar decided to continue his campaign without delay. Not
far from the frontier, at Barinas and at Rosario de
Cucuta, the Spaniards had gathered in considerable
force. This was a constant threat of invasion. The
Granadan Colonel Castillo had only three hundred
men with which to hold them in check, and he was relieved to hear of Bolivar's successes.

The latter wrote to President Torres asking for
authority to unite his troops with those of the province, and immediately equipped his force, five hundred men whom he selected with care, for the march
was to be a rough one; the Cordillera of the Andes
had to be crossed at a place reputed inaccessible. It
would be cold, and Bolivar's soldiers were all from
hot regions; thick clothes were issued to them. The
guns were packed on mules. All was ready for departure when the President's messenger arrived with
the permission. Half an hour later the battalion was
on its way.

There was first of all a desolate plain to be crossed, not a hut, not a human being. The only surprising things in this desert were natural walls of earth crowned by rare tufts of operetias. The rivers were dangerous because they were capable of overflowing in one night. A proverb says, 'Neither a stream before nor a load behind.' The camp woke sometimes in the middle of a lake. Moreover, there were no bridges, and fords had to be sought.

On the march they came across strange clefts in the earth. The swollen streams from the Cordilleras had ploughed up the ground. Towers of sand and clay, stalagmites and immense caverns were hollowed out. One would have said a country bewitched. It was often necessary to go back upon the track in order to skirt ravines that were too deep to cross. Bolivar did not allow these difficulties to trouble him. He had determined to cross the mountains, and cross he would.

Here at last were the first outposts of the Cordilleras, and at once the vegetation became gayer, richer; among ferns and bushes of pink flowers ran lizards as long as a man's arm.

Right up on the mountains, at more than three thousand metres' height, the army halted. The view was wonderful, the whole range was visible, overhanging the narrow valleys where flowed tumultuous streams. The blue of the horizon was hidden by the clouds which floated between the peaks.

The route became more and more dangerous.

There were only the precipitous paths called *angos-
turas*, on which two mules could not pass each other.
Stones rolled beneath the feet, and at every instant
there was danger of slipping to the bottom of the ravine. The Cordillera seemed interminable. Several
men, victims of a false step, could not be recovered.
Storms raged with unheard-of violence. The heights
flung back echoes of the thunder, and torrential rain
fell for hours together. The clothes which Bolivar had
distributed were not enough to protect the soldiers;
with their worn-out hats and scanty cloaks they were
obliged to shelter beneath rocks full of evil and unknown insects. But under these trials there was never
a word of discouragement. This colonel, not yet
thirty, spoke to his men with so much calmness and
courage that nobody dared to grumble.

There followed the abrupt descent of the opposite
slope, a descent even more difficult than the climb.
The men had constantly to cling to the branches; but
the army was so delighted to meet once more with
flowers, green grass, and singing birds that it thought
nothing of the danger.

With five hundred soldiers, in the middle of winter,
Bolivar had traversed a region where even the most
seasoned mountaineers dared not venture.

Barely time to reorganize and then a forced march
across the *llanos*, vast prairies broken by numerous
streams and verdant forests.

The Spaniards had no inkling of the surprise in

store for them. Some peasants, terrified at the sight
of this unlooked-for troop, gave warning of the arrival
of an army, doubtless considerable, from the south.
A panic followed.

Bolivar drove all before him, rejoined Castillo, who
had come by the northern route; with united forces
continued his advance and routed the enemy at Correa. The news of this victory had an excellent effect
upon the Government, who were beginning to mis-
trust the Venezuelan colonel's mad expeditions.

The booty was enormous. A million piastres'
worth of goods were sent to Cartagena.

But Bolivar found himself suddenly halted in the
moment of victory by the jealousy of the Granadan
commanders: Labatut, furious at being disobeyed,
and Castillo, full of envy, made protests to Cartagena.

Castillo made a very unfavourable report upon the
state of Bolivar's troops, maintaining that it was folly
to attack Venezuela under such conditions. It would
be leading the heroic citizens of New Granada to their
death. At Cartagena, Camillo Torres defended Bolivar, and obtained for him the rank of brigadier-general and military governor of Pamplona; but Castillo's friends intrigued so well that the order to start
was delayed and the Spaniards had time to re-form.

Hoping to placate Castillo, Bolivar entrusted him
with the pursuit of a Spanish detachment. Castillo
performed it successfully and became more presuming
than ever.

Labatut experienced a check at Santa Marta in the

north, and quitted New Granada, exiled by the assembly.

Castillo returned to Cartagena, taking the best units with him.

On this Bolivar assembled his men and addressed them:

'Soldiers, your arms have brought freedom to the gates of Venezuela. In less than two months you have accomplished two campaigns and you are about to begin a third which must end in my own country. True republicans, you are on your way to set free the Cradle of Liberty, as the Crusaders of old freed that of Christianity.

'As darkness scatters before the rays of the sun, the Spaniards will disappear at the mere sound of your guns.

'Brave soldiers, it is to your hands that America looks for salvation. Crown your proud name by winning renown as the saviours of Venezuela!'

Trujillo had been especially fortified by the Spaniards, who had made it into a stronghold of the highest order. Bolivar sent a dispatch to the President of the Union, declaring: 'I will await Your Excellency's reply at Trujillo.'

Bolivar possessed in all five hundred men and one hundred and forty thousand cartridges; he had as well four cannon, but only five shells. On the 15th of May, 1813, he left the village of San Cristóbal. The inhabitants of the country swelled his ranks. After a march through scenes of indescribable enthusiasm, Bolivar entered Trujillo on the 15th of June.

Wherever he passed, he addressed proclamations to the people inviting them to shake off the royalist yoke and join him. Volunteers streamed in.

Leaving four hundred men with José Felix Rivas, he fell upon the enemy, whom he took in the rear and put to flight. He rejoined Rivas, who on his side had won some five victories, and, drunk with success, the two armies united their efforts.

XIX

In the mean time a republican fleet, commanded by the Italian adventurer Bianchi, had appeared off Cumaná with transports bringing Mariño's army. The Spaniards were blockaded and in danger of a landing at any moment. At Maturin, Piar had won a great victory over Monteverde in person.

Who was to be the first to enter Caracas?

Bolivar advanced like lightning; nobody withstood him, the Spaniards fled at his approach without even showing fight. He wished to have the honour of delivering the capital with his own hand.

The Spanish Major Izquierdo received orders to bar his way. Izquierdo had formidable artillery; he took up a position on the plain of Taguanes.

Bolivar and his lancers charged at the gallop, the infantry followed at the double. The Spaniards were in close column protected by their guns. The republican attack was twenty times renewed; bullets made terrible havoc in their ranks and there was a slight movement of withdrawal. Bolivar and his two lieutenants, Rivas and Girardot, rushed to the head of their troops and at last repulsed the enemy, who fell back upon a wooded hill. If once the Spaniards could gain this height, they would be safe, for from the cover of the trees they might fire unmolested.

Bolivar gave orders that every rider should take a foot-soldier on his crupper and cut off Izquierdo's retreat. As they went, the infantry discharged their muskets at the Spaniards, who, caught between two fires, were quickly disposed of. Izquierdo was killed. In the fury of the fight the wounded were finished off with bayonets. At midnight it was seen that not a Spaniard remained alive upon the battle-field of Taguanes.

Alarmed by this news, Monteverde sought refuge at Puerto Cabello.

The Governor of Caracas came to treat for surrender. He had brought with him the Marquis of Casa-León and Iturbe, men to whom Bolivar owed everything. Confronted with such an embassy, Bolivar showed his gratitude; he undertook to respect the Spaniards' property, and called on them to leave Venezuela, giving a month to allow for the removal of all their possessions. He authorized the garrisons to keep their arms and colours. He wished his generosity to be a reply to the brutality with which the Spaniards had violated the treaty signed by Miranda.

But this capitulation had to be ratified by Monteverde, who, still shut up in Puerto Cabello, refused to treat with those whom he termed traitors and rebels. He was implored to save a multitude of lives by his signature, but he would not give way.

At La Guayra the number of fugitives was so great that many overloaded boats were sunk. Those who could not leave the port were imprisoned. There were a thousand of them, who were kept as hostages.

On the 6th of August, Bolivar entered Caracas.

The sight of his native town which he had left in such a state of desolation moved him to hot tears. Garlands and draperies in the republican colours hung from every window. Bolivar in full-dress uniform marched at the head of his troops followed by his staff. In his hand he held a baton set with stars of gold, the token of supreme command. Bells pealed, trumpets blared, and guns fired blank cartridges without intermission. In the streets the people cheered the conquerors. Bolivar was compelled to mount a chariot covered with laurel and drawn by twelve charming young women crowned with flowers.

The soldiers, who in spite of their youth and lack of experience had just shown themselves superior to the veterans of Spain, marched past, barefoot for the most part, clothed in rags, covered with wounds, but smiling. The enthusiasm was redoubled when they displayed the flags taken from the enemy.

In the market-place the notables of the town welcomed Bolivar, and bestowed on him the title of 'Libertador.'

XX

BOLIVAR decorated the bravest of his men with the 'Order of Liberators.' He addressed the assembly in refusal of the dictatorship which had been offered him: if he had helped them to victory, he had not been the only one to do it (he pointed to the glorious wounded men of his escort). He would see that the laws were obeyed, but it was not for him to make them; the representatives of the people were charged with that duty.

But Bolivar was urged with such insistence that in the end he accepted; only yielding that he might accomplish his work of independence, free to give up his title as soon as peace was restored. Alas, this peace depended not alone upon victories over the enemy. The gravest trouble often sprang from such successes.

Mariño, coöperating with Bianchi's fleet and the troops under Piar, had succeeded in taking Cumaná; he had massacred some hundreds of prisoners because he had not time to secure them. He had sunk five Spanish ships, and appointed himself supreme lord and dictator of eastern Venezuela. He did not choose to obey Bolivar.

Antonio Briceño, deputy of Caracas, driven mad by the cruelties of the Spaniards towards his family, raised a band of fanatics and almost without weapons exterminated all whom he believed to be in sympathy with the enemy. He fell into an ambush and was executed. The death of this lunatic was a relief to every one, but cost some good men their lives.

In spite of his title of Dictator, Bolivar was not supreme. The republican troops were for the most part mere bands commanded by ambitious and unscrupulous adventurers fighting in their own interest rather than that of the country. Every conqueror fancied himself a king, and would no longer acknowledge the authority of the Commander-in-Chief. The most sweeping victories were always discounted by personal quarrels. Bolivar had to act with finesse, to flatter the presuming and promise a great deal in order to get a moderate amount of help. No one man is strong enough to dominate all the others. The most difficult thing in this war was to make the different nationalities realize that they were all part of the same country: that this was a war of principle, to win freedom from the Spaniards, and that they must devote themselves to the cause of liberty. Bolivar redoubled his proclamations, he addressed his men every day; but the fortunes of war are changeable, and with them went the convictions of those who had been considered most trustworthy. On both sides alike desertions multiplied at the slightest check, and a small reverse might spread to a disaster.

Thanks to a forced loan of one hundred and twenty thousand piastres, which the Spanish merchants in Caracas had been compelled to contribute, Bolivar was able to organize his army to his liking. For a long time he had dreamt of a uniform designed by himself, and when his troops took the road on the 20th of August they were at last dressed alike.

Bolivar's aim was to dislodge Monteverde from Puerto Cabello. The place was a very bitter memory to him, because he had left while it was still intact. Halfway there, however, he was obliged to detail two of his columns to put down risings organized by the Curé Torrelas in the Indian villages. He resumed his march with diminished forces.

On August 25th, Girardot seized the outermost works; Bolivar had all his guns mounted there and gave the order to bombard Puerto Cabello. A general attack failed, but the Spanish Major Zuazola, renowned for his cruelty, was made prisoner. Bolivar proposed to Monteverde to exchange him for a patriot officer detained in the citadel. Monteverde refused, and Zuazola was hanged in front of the ramparts.

The rather serious losses which his army had suffered compelled Bolivar to raise the siege. He quartered himself at Valencia to refresh his troops.

Monteverde, who had been reënforced and who considered Bolivar's retreat to be a sign of weakness, flung himself in pursuit. They joined battle on the heights of Barula. The enemy was hurled back, but as Girardot was in the act of planting his colours on a hill which he had just carried at the point of the bayonet, a bullet struck him full in the forehead.

Bolivar, who felt the spirit of his men begin to ebb, had Girardot's heart placed in a silver casket. The Granadans, in revenge for their leader, begged Bolivar to trust to them alone the task of charging the enemy. With wild fury they fell upon the Spaniards and gave no quarter. Monteverde himself was seriously wounded and had to be carried off the field by his aides-de-camp.

After this victory, Bolivar returned to Caracas, where a magnificent reception had been prepared for him. His title of 'Liberator' was reaffirmed, this time officially by the Assembly, who bestowed it as a 'tribute of the national gratitude to the bravest son of Venezuela.'

XXI

FIRST a servant, afterwards skipper of a boat, a smuggler, implicated in some shady affair and condemned by the authorities at Puerto Cabello to eight years' imprisonment, Boves was released by the Spaniards on condition that he fight against the revolutionaries.

He was a short man, as broad as he was long, with deep-set, light-coloured eyes, a nose like an eagle's beak, ruddy skin, bristly hair and beard, and the strength of Hercules; Boves raised bands of herdsmen, the *llaneros*. War was his delight; he would have fought as happily against no matter whom; it was a means for assuaging his thirst for blood. Extremely brave, moreover, and always in the van of his 'infernal legion' brandishing a blood-stained flag, he was wounded at least thirty times. Never would he admit defeat; beaten by Bolivar, having saved only ten men out of his fifteen hundred riders, he remade a fresh army. When he entered a village, the folk were obliged to obey him; they had heard of his cruelty and were afraid.

In a deserted town where no one remained save an old man and a child, he gave orders to behead the man.

'Spare him,' implored the boy, 'and I will be your slave.'

'I will spare him if you will let your ears and nose be cut off without a cry.'

The boy did not utter a cry.

'Kill the old man, he is a traitor; and as for the boy, kill him too; in a few years he would be able to fight against us.'

On the Venezuelan side there was only one man as savage as Boves: Campo Elias. He had left his wife and children to give himself without reserve to the joy of killing Spaniards. He succeeded one day in meeting Boves; it was his highest hope.

The battle was so furious that out of all his army Boves alone escaped, covered with wounds. Campo Elias put to the sword all the inhabitants of a town because they had not revolted against Boves. A month later, Boves took an abundant revenge and it was Campo Elias's turn to flee.

Many other Spanish officers were no better than Boves. Morales, always followed by a gigantic executioner, Rosete, known as the 'Captain'; quartering, hanging, burning, flaying, and the most terrifying tortures were his amusements. Zuazola wore in his hat the ear of a republican. Antonanzas ripped open pregnant women, wreaked his madness on the bodies, and pushed his sadism to the length of sending his friends boxes full of hands and fragments of flesh. He built pyramids of skulls and bones. Massacres bred massacres.

Boves boasted that he had with his own hands slaughtered three hundred persons in one afternoon.

His men feared him, for when he was drunk he would just as soon have killed his own soldiers if they showed any disapproval.

Monteverde's chaplain, Eusebio de Coronil, a fanatical Capuchin, recommended that no Venezuelan over seven years old should be left alive.

Yanes carried about with him an iron with which he branded the prisoners before he killed them.

The lust for blood reached a point which could not be exceeded. The republicans themselves ended by giving way to it. A general who hated his Spanish origin murdered his whole family, and declared that he would commit suicide for the sole purpose of doing away with a man of royalist birth.

Boves had collected a formidable troop of horse, composed of bandits set free from the hulks and *llaneros*, who, being no longer able to live on the produce of their cattle-breeding, found it easier to plunder.

Advancing with his irresistible legion, Boves fought twice against Bolivar. His intervention in the wars of independence had more the appearance of personal vengeance than of Spanish repression. Bolivar, who was obliged to treat the inhabitants kindly, was short of stores; Boves, on the contrary, stole the treasures of the churches and seized the goods of private people: his horsemen had abundance of everything and ended by enjoying the charms of a dangerous but profitable existence.

Bolivar lost nearly one thousand men at La Puerta.

In spite of acts of heroism, such as that of Ricaurte, who waited to blow himself up until the Spaniards had surrounded him, and then, setting fire to the powder magazine, took with him to his death a number of the royalists — in spite of the courage of all his lieutenants, Bolivar was condemned to beat a retreat.

Mariño, roused at last from his silence, fell into a snare set by Boves, and, flinging his infantry against that of the enemy, found it rapidly surrounded by horsemen whom the woods had concealed. Bolivar could only estimate the extent of the disaster. Mariño fell back off Cumaná. Bolivar gave up Caracas, since he could no longer hold it. Thousands of people followed him to escape the persecutions which were bound to ensue. The roads were choked with girls, children, women, and priests carrying whatever they held most dear. A great many perished through terror, fever, or privation.

The news of the enemy's cruelty decided even the most resigned. At Aragua hundreds of civilian refugees in a church were murdered to the last soul in the presence of the Holy Sacrament, and, as the Spaniards had not time to bury them, the town was set on fire.

People fled by thousands amid scenes of panic, confusion, and consternation.

XXII

BOLIVAR's secretary, engaged in opening the letters, turned towards his master.

'General, here is a letter from the Governor of La Guayra. He has only five hundred men, and the prisons contain as many Spaniards. He has not forgotten the treachery at Puerto Cabello, and fears a plot. He asks for instructions.'

Bolivar had just posted up an appeal to all citizens from twelve to sixty years of age.

'In our present situation I cannot hesitate. Be good enough to write the following answer':

To José Leandro Palacios, Commandant of La Guayra:
Your despatch of the 4th, which has just reached me, informs me of the critical situation in which you are. You have not enough men and have in your custody a considerable number of prisoners. In consequence of this I order you to put to death immediately all the Spaniards who are in the cells or in the hospital buildings, without any exception.

SIMON BOLIVAR

HEADQUARTERS OF THE LIBERATOR AT VALENCIA
February 8, 1814, 8 *o'clock* P.M.

Bolivar had pilloried the excesses of Briceño, who wrote letters in blood, and who graded his rewards in the following order:

10 Spanish heads: rank of ensign.
30 Spanish heads: rank of lieutenant.
50 Spanish heads: rank of captain.

He was forced now to realize that horrors must be repaid by other horrors. The abominable crimes committed by Monteverde's troops cried out for vengeance; there was an unending history of fresh massacres, and the Venezuelan soldiers, who knew that their families had suffered torture, no longer spared the royalists who fell into their hands.

Bolivar himself, driven beyond endurance, decreed 'War to the death.' 'Every inhabitant of the country who takes up arms for the enemy or helps him in any way whatsoever will be executed.'

At La Guayra the Governor had hardly received Bolivar's reply before he gave orders to shoot all the prisoners; but powder and shot cost money — they were killed with lances and swords.

The last feelings of pity gave way before a fury of violence. The half-castes, who came of savage blood, felt rise within them the most brutal instincts of their forbears. The nobles even exceeded them in ferocity. Arismendi was a terror to the Spaniards. His young wife had been taken captive and sent to Cadiz, where in the prison she gave birth to 'a new monster' as her jailers called it. She was promised her freedom if she would persuade her husband to desert.

'Kill me as well as my child,' she said, 'but my husband's duty is to exterminate you.'

It was no longer a time for such generous acts as that of a Venezuelan commander who, having offered to exchange his Spanish captives for republican prisoners, and finding his proposal scouted, released the Spaniards loaded with kindness, in order to show that a patriot had more greatness of mind than his oppressors.

No one surrendered now. They fought to the last gasp, for they knew what fate awaited them.

But Bolivar, who sent out orders for execution signed with his name, was anxious in spite of everything to clear himself. He wrote a manifesto to the people of the Old World: he related the atrocities of which his compatriots had been the victims; he waxed eloquent in his description of the barbarities of the Spaniards, who had not even the excuse of fighting for justice. If he was forced to retaliate by terrible means, which were repugnant to him, it was solely to deliver his country from a shameful and blood-stained tyranny.

XXIII

MISFORTUNES rained upon the Liberator. Taking refuge with Mariño at Cumaná, he arranged for the emigration of all the civil population to the island of Margarita, which was easier to defend. The Italian Bianchi and his pirates were to carry out the transfer. Bolivar trusted them, and sent them the treasure which he had managed to save.

In the darkness of night, Bianchi fled with the treasure, all the weapons, the guns, and the ammunition which he was to have taken to Margarita. Accompanied by Mariño, Bolivar leapt into a brig, hoisted all sail, and overtook the pirates on the high seas. Bianchi merely replied:

'I do not make war for my amusement. I snap my fingers at Venezuelans and Spaniards both. I was promised forty thousand piastres and I have had nothing. I cannot wait for ever. My men are sick of promises which seldom seem to be binding.'

After a long argument, Bianchi agreed to restore part of the treasure and to cast anchor off Margarita. Bolivar and Mariño landed on the island, where utter confusion reigned; they stayed only for a few hours and returned to the mainland. As they were entering a house at Carupaño, they were arrested and taken before a triumvirate consisting of Piar, Rivas, and Bermudez. Bolivar and Mariño were accused of having fled before the enemy, abandoned their army,

THE EMIGRATION OF 1814

and carried off the treasure with the connivance of Bianchi.

The latter, hearing that Bolivar and Mariño were to be imprisoned, arrived before Carupaño, came ashore himself, and ordered the release of the two former dictators, saying that otherwise he would bombard the town. Rivas was obliged to submit, but Bolivar pardoned him for what might have been an heroic and sincere action; he resigned his power in his favour, and set out with Mariño a second time for Curaçao.

The second Venezuelan republic had run its course. Rivas, still wearing his cap of liberty, was captured and executed by the Spaniards. His head was exhibited as d'España's had been in an iron cage. Bermudez had the glory of killing Boves, but was obliged to seek refuge abroad.

In the desert regions of the south the remaining chiefs carried on a guerrilla existence for some time.

Only ruins and corpses remained.

XXIV

BEFORE he was killed by the thrust of a lance, Boves had done the greatest harm to the republican cause. Without his fury and his perfidy the Spaniards would assuredly have been beaten. When he seized Valencia, he pushed his treachery to the point of himself proposing very favourable terms for surrender. He had Mass said, and swore before the altar that he would observe the treaty. That night he gave a great ball to celebrate the peace which was at last imminent. All the nobility were invited and could do nothing else but go. At midnight the lights went out and all the dancers from the town were murdered. Boves sent Cajigal a letter to tell him of this pretty success: 'General, I believe that this will be enough to compensate for your reserves.'

Cajigal, who had no self-respect, sent him a colonel's commission, which Boves sent back to him, saying: 'I have already made a tolerable lot of colonels myself.'

Before he died, Boves declared: 'There is only one thing that annoys me, and that is to be replaced by Morales. The man disgusts me; he is too blood-thirsty. . . . I am sorry, too, that I have not managed to kill Bolivar. I believe that I should have struck him down even in a tabernacle. However, one cannot do everything.'

If Boves had been killed three months earlier, the

fate of Venezuela would certainly have been very different, and Bolivar would not have been obliged to sail for Curaçao, where, however, he did not remain. He was in too great haste to report to the Assembly at Cartagena the unfavourable conditions which had forced him to abandon the struggle.

On the 1st of December, he presented himself before the heads of the Government. He explained that the insurrection of the province of Caracas had been fatal to him, as he had always predicted; the lack of munitions, of arms, and of provisions had not been compensated by personal bravery.

New Granada was in danger. The authorities knew Bolivar's military capacity and commissioned him at once to take the head of a contingent and pacify the province of Bogotá, which was divided against itself and refused to submit to Cartagena.

Bolivar wished to avoid a civil war. He knew that Santa Fé de Bogotá was a republican town whose pride had no doubt been ruffled; she must be brought back to right thinking without any shedding of blood. With great tact Bolivar wrote to the Dictator Alvarez, pointing out the horrors of a fratricidal war. Alvarez did all that he could to stir up the popular fury against Bolivar, but the people would not hear him and preferred to surrender.

On the steps of the cathedral at Bogotá, Bolivar made a speech which ended thus:

'Let us forget internal feuds; the existence of New

Granada is gravely threatened. We must all unite to strive against the invader.'

While Bolivar, taught by experience, was planning a new offensive against the Spaniards, an odious pamphlet was circulated against him. It said that Bolivar had been the death of thousands of Granadans in order to recover his own estates. The affair of Bianchi reappeared, distorted, till it showed Bolivar as an ignoble traitor. All these attacks were organized by General Castillo, who could not yet forgive the predominant place taken by a Venezuelan in the army of Granada.

Castillo had influence at Cartagena. Bolivar, wishing to put an end to these jealousies, claimed for Castillo the rank of brigadier-general.

There began to be talk of a formidable fleet which the Spanish had sent against the Tierra Firme, and whose appearance could not be long delayed. Bolivar asked himself whether his presence in New Granada and the dissensions which it might provoke was not harmful to the peace of the country. If he were gone, would not the Granadans unite in face of the enemy?

On the 1st of May he embarked, after having sent out a final proclamation:

'... *Granadans and Venezuelans:*
'I see myself compelled to leave you, you who have gone with me through so many vicissitudes and who have been my companions in arms in so many battles.

I part from you to live in inactivity without even the hope of offering my life to my country.

'My grief is terrible; in renouncing the right to lead you, as of old, to victory, I sacrifice my heart, my fortune, and my glory. But the fate of the country lays this duty upon me, and I cannot hesitate. I do not wish to be a source of difficulty and strife, which can only delay the necessary action; it is for me to go. The salvation of all is in your hands, it is on you that the prosperity of the Revolution depends. Be proud of it and do your best. The task which falls to you is the finest task there is. Farewell.'

On the 1st of May, the port of Cartagena was gay. Nothing would make one suspect that there was a war, that such terrible events had so lately taken place, and that so many others were on the way. On the ships the sailors sang as they hoisted the sails. Bolivar did not know yet where he should go. His secretary Mendez went with him. The boat left harbour slowly, rounding the lighthouses of the two ports.

Bolivar was on the quarter-deck, motionless, his eyes fixed on that well-known coast, which grew fainter and more faint and in a few minutes had faded into the horizon.

XXV

In Jamaica, Bolivar led an existence like that which he had formerly led at Curaçao. He was scarcely any richer, but he was more famous. Hospitality was offered him and people went so far as to lend him a house.

Bolivar used to work there all day long. He received news of the war: Venezuela was completely occupied by the Spaniards and New Granada gravely menaced.

If Castillo and the others were fighting sword in hand, it could not be said that he on his part would not help the cause of independence. He spread out his maps on a big table which he had placed in the verandah. He calculated the number of inhabitants in all the South American countries and what could be hoped from them; he made a scheme for the union of New Granada and Venezuela under the name of Colombia, in gratitude to Christopher Columbus: a town was to be founded between the two countries and called Las Casas, after the 'Father of the Indians.' Seven millions of people asked only to be free, and the day which would bring them liberty was inevitably coming. It would have been base to give up all idea of relief.

Bolivar wrote proclamations and articles which he sent to France, the United States, and England. He tried to interest the whole universe in his plans; he pointed out that the best form of government for the New World would have been a republic with a president elected for life, and an hereditary senate which would have served as a link between leader and people. Bolivar already saw his country free; he was aglow with the idea. Mendez, more prudent, listened to him without speaking, approved, but with less confidence than his master.

One day Bolivar heard that an influential Englishman, who was sympathetic towards the Venezuelans, had just landed on the island. At an early hour he left his house, which was right in the country, to go and interview this man. Their conversation was lengthy, and rather than go home Bolivar took a room in an hotel at the port, so as to sleep there.

Meanwhile, one of Bolivar's friends had come to see him at his own house. Bolivar had warned no one of his departure, and the friend, who was tired after the long ride, stretched himself in the hammock to wait for him, and ended by falling asleep.

In the middle of the night some one entered by the window, cautiously approached the hammock, and stabbed the sleeper several times, then fled; but in climbing down he made a false step and fell. The servants, waking in alarm, sprang up, saw a shadow fleeing through the garden, gave chase, and caught him. It was an Indian slave who admitted that he had taken money from a Spanish Jew to kill Bolivar; but the Jew was no longer in Jamaica; the police searched in vain, nothing was discovered. The slave was condemned to be hanged.

Returning the next day, Bolivar found his friend, by what an unbelievable chance, killed in his stead; it was a long time before he could blot the picture from his mind.

There was in Jamaica a shipowner in search of adventure, an eccentric Frenchman, rich, moreover, and the owner of a veritable fleet: Brion by name. He struck up friendship with Bolivar, warmed to his opinions, and, whether from hope of gain or from motives of pure chivalry, he offered his ships to the Venezuelan. Bolivar wished to convey provisions to Cartagena, from which came worse and worse news. Castillo had been accused of treason and degraded from his rank, and Morillo, the Spanish general, had arrived with all his fleet and decided to blockade the coast and lay siege to Cartagena.

At the very moment of departure, Bolivar heard that Cartagena had just fallen into the hands of the enemy. This place, which he believed impregnable, had given way as soon as he left it.

XXVI

NEVER had the Spaniards sent so formidable an army to America as that commanded by Morillo: ten thousand five hundred men, first-class artillery, and three-decker battleships.

An explosion nearly cost the general his life; one of the largest frigates blew up with nine hundred men, but this unfortunate beginning did not prevent Morillo from taking possession of Cartagena, where he found nothing but ruins and rotting corpses. Famine even more than bombardment had conquered the besieged city.

Nevertheless, Bolivar left Jamaica; he took with him all the patriots on the island and set sail for Hayti; on the way he fell in with two Spanish brigs, which were captured by boarding.

In Hayti, Bolivar was kindly received by the negro President Pétion. Fêtes were given in his honour. This nation of revolted slaves, who had beaten Rochambeau, looked with a favourable eye on every attempt to rise against the Europeans. Pétion offered Bolivar a number of guns, barrels of powder, and shells.

On February 6th, there arrived at Cayes a boat which had managed to cheat the vigilance of the Spaniards and which bore all the surviving leaders from Cartagena: Piar, Mariño, Bermudez, the Scots-

man MacGregor, and several others. Bolivar informed them that he meant to attack Venezuela from
the eastern coast, using for base the island of Margarita, which still held out against the Spaniards.
Bolivar was invested with every authority, civil and
military.

On the 3d of May, the patriot army, which contained more field officers than privates, cast anchor
off Margarita. The islanders, who were all giants full
of admirable courage, had successfully repulsed two
attacks by Morillo.

After a fortnight's preparation, Bolivar weighed
anchor and laid siege to Carupaño, which he took
without much difficulty. As he walked past the
prison, he remarked to Piar and Bermudez:

'Do you remember the time when you would have
liked to have me shut up in this place? I bear you no
malice, for I know that you were sincere and that my
disappearance may well have seemed suspicious. I
left Cumaná only to overtake Bianchi and recover
from him the treasure and ammunition which we
needed.'

'General, will you ever forgive us for the ill-con-
sidered action which we took against you? The agita-
tion was so great that we had not time to inquire into
suspicious circumstances.'

'Piar and Bermudez, all that is forgotten. You
acted like resolute patriots, and I am only sorry that
poor Rivas is not also here, that I might tell him too

THE EXPEDITION OF LES CAYES: BOARDING THE BRIGANTINE INTRÉPIDO

what sympathy I felt for all three of you when you decided to condemn me.'

Piar and Mariño were commissioned to recruit the greatest possible number of men. The slaves were set free, which did not at all please the rich owners, but an army had to be raised by hook or by crook.

Soublette, who had ventured into the valley of Aragua with a weak contingent, was defeated by Morales.

Bolivar had all the munitions embarked in his remaining boats. He was awaked one night by the news that the enemy's fleet was at hand. Without hesitation he took to the open sea, intending to put in at Asuncion in Margarita, but while at sea a storm overtook him, and, being at the same time pursued by a strong enemy squadron, he returned to Hayti, to Port au Prince.

Arismendi, who was still defending Margarita, besought him to come to their help. Bolivar bought twelve thousand guns and landed on the island on December 28, 1816.

The situation was hopeful once again. Piar, whose army amounted now to fifteen hundred men, was marching towards Guiana, after having subdued the provinces of Barcelona. MacGregor at the head of three hundred horse had overrun two hundred leagues and had beaten General Morales. Mariño had taken several villages on the coast.

But the best news was the recruiting of the *llaneros* by General Paez. After Boves's death the *llaneros* of the 'infernal legion' had no leader capable of commanding them. Badly paid by the Spaniards, many had gone back to their plains. It was then that Paez had the idea of winning them for the republican cause.

Paez, a man of the people, badly educated, but of a courage and resolution that were the admiration of Venezuela, was the only man who could have succeeded with the *llaneros*. These remarkable horsemen, accustomed from childhood to train wild horses, and armed with lances to protect their herds from savage beasts, were to become under Paez one of the most formidable units of the Venezuelan army. Scarcely civilized, Indians, half-castes, toughened by the hardships of their life, they were as one with their horses. Their lances, whose light and flexible wooden shafts were ten feet long, ended in great blades with cutting edges. The charge of these lancers was irresistible, but it needed a hand of iron to keep them in order.

Paez, having heard that a rider had been found looting, had him brought before him:

'Send every one out; and now you — brigand — take off your coat and hat, as I do. I might have had you shot, but you do not deserve even that, so look out for your skin.'

Grappling with the *llanero*, he flung him to the ground; the other tried to hit back, but Paez administered a thorough thrashing.

'Dress yourself. I think that you have had enough for to-day, and do not let it happen again.'

Paez at length acquired such power over this cavalry that he got surprising results from them. He was the god that no one dared resist.

Morillo step by step was conquering the whole of New Granada; Bolivar replied by seizing Guiana.

Finding himself one day with but fifteen men, and having decided to join forces with Piar, Bolivar assembled his small escort and announced to them:

'We have to cross a large district under enemy occupation, and we must cross it at all costs. No weakness will be tolerated.' And he set off.

As he rounded a wood, he fell in with a Spanish column. Drawing his sword, he sprang forward and cried:

'First battalion to the right, second to the left. Chasseurs, follow me!'

The Spaniards thought that they had to deal with the patriot army and fled. Bolivar at a gallop made a feint of pursuing them, but turned aside into a wood. He stayed there for a whole day. At night he had to cross the Orinoco, swollen by the floods. Bolivar found a little boat, waited for the darkness, took no one with him but his secretary Mendez, left their two horses with his companions, whom he ordered to turn back, and in absolute silence rowed towards the other shore.

No sooner was he ashore than he plunged into the undergrowth. It was high time, for twenty Spaniards were already close to the canoe. Bolivar and Mendez crawled to a glade where they saw the horses of their pursuers; they unfastened two of them and fled for their lives. Some shots rang out, but the Venezuelans were already far away.

Two days later they reached Piar's camp, still in front of Angostura.

XXVII

With the help of Madariaga, an incorrigible chatter-box escaped from prison at Cadiz, and a canon to boot, Mariño had, in Bolivar's absence, set up a federal government. Naturally he had appointed himself Commander-in-Chief, and he sent a message to Bolivar summoning him to come and recognize the new triumvirate. Bolivar answered that he would not recognize anything, and that in any case he had not time to come.

A fortnight, moreover, was enough to abolish the claims of Mariño, whose circle ended by laughing at him. But Piar, annoyed with Bolivar's importance and the blame which he had received for his inaction before Angostura, rebelled openly, and declared that he would obey no one but Mariño. Bolivar summoned him. Piar had already fled. General Cedeño was sent off upon his heels with orders to bring him back dead or alive.

Bolivar took the operations into his own hands. He had boats built, and with the coöperation of Brion's flotilla, which had at last succeeded in getting up the Orinoco River, he gave the word to attack. The garrison of Angostura attempted to steal away on the Spanish vessels, which were heavy and little adapted for river navigation. Brion harassed them with *flecheros*, and the Spaniards had great difficulty in escaping as far as the island of Grenada, a British possession, where they were disarmed.

Bolivar was master of the most important port on the Orinoco. With his light squadrons he kept the enemy on the *qui vive* as far as the eastern frontier. The whole system of rivers was in his possession.

Morillo, who believed that the core of resistance was still at Margarita, attempted a third landing, after sending first terms and then threats. He was repulsed by General Gomez, who had no idea of handing over the island to the Spaniards.

At this point Morillo heard of Bolivar's victories and used them as an excuse for quitting that cursed spot where he could never bring anything off.

Piar was arrested and brought to Angostura before Bolivar, who had him locked up. A court-martial was called, composed of Brion, president; Generals Pedro Léon Torres, Anzoategui, and Soublette and various colonels and lieutenant-colonels, all tried men, whose resolution was only equalled by their courage. Piar did not even attempt to defend himself; he was accused of having tried to divide the army under the pretext of colour hatred so as to seize the sole power for himself. He was unanimously condemned to capital punishment.

He was shot at dawn.

Bolivar had insisted on being present at the execution; he made a speech to the troops:

'This day is a day of mourning for my heart, but General Piar was a traitor and a deserter. A just and lawfully appointed court has pronounced his sentence of death.

'General Piar has rendered great services, but he had none the less become a danger to the republic.

'We have broken the fetters of your slavery; it must not be said that one of ourselves attacked the common freedom.

'As I have been present at your triumphs so have I shared your dangers and misfortunes.

'Rely on me, and be sure that you will always find in me as much love as if I were your own father.'

This severe measure, rendered necessary by the ambitious action of a general who was brave, but of only moderate intelligence, was nevertheless most painful to Bolivar, who still dreamed of freeing his country by kindness and not by force.

XXVIII

Out of men whom nothing had called to a military career, Bolivar succeeded in making excellent soldiers. Negroes, half-castes, Indians, Creoles, French, and English, race mattered little.

Apart from his undeniable ability as a tactician who knew how to profit by the lay of the land and who had been the first to realize what sort of war he would have to wage, he possessed in the highest degree the gift of command. His rough and clear voice, the energy with which he overcame fatigue and fever, his authority and his tact, when he felt it called for, made him at once the Generalissimo. The most mutinous of his officers were obliged to admit his superiority; Mariño, after his deplorable attacks and reverses, was to come and ask forgiveness; Paez, looked on as a god by his own men, was to put them none the less at Bolivar's disposal. All were struck by the administrative power of this man whom nothing escaped, who in order to make canteens for his soldiers collected everything that was made of beaten brass, and iron wire cages. They lacked solder. One day Bolivar tore his breeches on a nail, examined it and found that it was of tin; all the tin nails in the town were requisitioned that same day. He noticed the smallest details, designed the uniform, tried several sorts of horseshoe to decide upon the soundest and most economical. And that was nothing. Scarcely was a

battle over before he was writing articles which he
sent to the European papers, drawing up proclamations, establishing laws, presiding at meetings, making most absorbing plans, and amidst this exhausting
life finding time to dance for hours and to think of women. How often did he tear himself from the arms of
a casual mistress to rush into battle! Two days later,
it would be another woman that he took with him in
his retreat or his offensive. His soldiers were no more
chaste than himself, taking on their campaigns fan-
tastic creatures who called themselves *rabonas* or
cantinieras, and who sometimes mixed in the fighting
with terrible ferocity.

But above all his manly and intellectual qualities,
Bolivar possessed that of knowing how to raise enthusiasm. Many of his soldiers would have suffered
torture rather than betray him.

Once, when in order to avoid falling into the hands
of the enemy he was obliged to take to the water and
swim, he saw one of his men who had followed him
and who was swimming with difficulty because of an
enormous knife which he would on no account let go.

'What's that knife for?' asked Bolivar.

'To kill you, sir; if the Spaniards should seize you,
they shall not get you alive.'

Bolivar has been blamed for the affair of Girardot's
heart, which he put into a silver urn, but at a moment
when their courage seemed to be faltering it was an
excellent way to put spirit into his men.

At Virijima, Colonel Villapol was killed and his men

seemed to be very much upset by the loss. Bolivar summoned Captain Ortega, under fire, and said:

'You know what this means — commander of Villapol's division?' Then, turning towards the infantry:

'You have no right to mourn for your leader till you have avenged him.'

Every battalion had an emblem and a name. Before the battle of Araure a new batch of recruits begged for a title.

'You shall have nothing till you have proved yourselves; the others have earned their names. I shall wait for you.'

The recruits gave way before the enemies' first push. Bolivar ordered them to be disarmed:

'Soldiers of the "nameless battalion," if you wish for arms and flags, go and find them.'

The young Venezuelans, armed only with sticks and stones, fell on the Spaniards with such a fury that nothing could stop them. They picked up whatever they found, guns or swords, and fought with such fine spirit that the Spaniards were scattered.

From the top of a hill the Liberator had been a quiet observer of the scene. When the battle was unquestionably won, he congratulated the 'nameless battalion.'

'Keep the colours of the royal regiment of Numancia which you have just defeated. You will call yourselves henceforward "the victors of Araure." I am pleased with you.'

THE BATTLE OF ARAURE

It was often thanks to words like these that Bolivar, at the head of a scanty column untrained and badly equipped, came to rout the best regular troops of Ferdinand VII.

XXIX

November 10, 1817.

At Angostura, Bolivar opened the session of the Council of State.

'When the Venezuelan nation for the first time broke with Spain, her first care was to establish a constitution and a federal republic.

'The fortune of war was against us and the constitution was destroyed by the enemy. We were then so preoccupied with military matters, going from one province to another and never ceasing to fight, that no time was left us to reconsider Constitutions. The disorder was so great that a dictatorship was necessary. I suffered more than any one from the anarchy and the obligation for unrelenting rigour, but I was watching for a moment of stability in which to give you laws. There may have been a head of the Government, but on the other hand there were neither judges nor deputies.

'It is wise to watch for a chance to reëstablish them.

'The Council of State will have legislative powers and will be consulted before any execution of Government orders.

'The High Court of Justice will, if necessary, protect innocent citizens against the supreme ruler.

Their rights will be safeguarded from the despotism or the caprice of a mere official.

'A Chamber of Commerce will take charge of the possibilities of trade and the speedy return to agriculture and industry.

'All the liberated provinces are thoroughly organized against any Spanish attack; the farmers are going back to their fields, and already some of the villages seem to have recovered from the war.

'General Monagas and General Bermudez will defend the frontiers which we have just defined.

'The island of Margarita, whose inhabitants have shown an extremely fine example of courage, will be the first to receive food and ammunition. She has repulsed every attack of General Morillo and has suffered terrible damage. Admiral Brion is commissioned to provision her generously. Gratitude prompts us to this elementary duty.

'General Paez has been able to recall the *llaneros* to patriotism, he has made them realize that they were led astray.

'The province of Guiana being the first liberated will receive the same constitution that the whole of Venezuela, let us hope, will have some day; three departments with civil and military codes which I have prepared in detail. General Sedeño will be commissioned to defend this province. I put at his disposal two squadrons of cavalry, two infantry battalions, two batteries of artillery, and the National Guard.

'An Executive Council will be appointed to deal

with all foreign relations and the purchase of munitions, and in case of death of an existing ruler, to
elect his successor.

'We all appreciate the energy and courage displayed by our brave soldiers. I demand that the national wealth be distributed to reward them for the
services they have rendered.

'Until Caracas is delivered, Angostura will remain
the capital of Venezuela.

'Venezuela is a Christian country; it is therefore
necessary to convoke an ecclesiastical assembly to
pronounce on the free practice of the Faith and on all
religious questions.

'I consider that, protected as she now is by well-
equipped troops, possessing upright magistrates and
judges and an honoured Council of State, our province should be able to withstand every attack.'

Bolivar was anxious to resume command of the
military operations as soon as possible, since he knew
that in his absence the generals could not always co-
ordinate their efforts, or turn them to account. He
pushed on the preparations with so much speed that
on December 31st he was able to take the field with a
considerable army.

'Bolivar.'
'Paez! At last we meet; it has been my wish for a
long time. I am greatly pleased with your way of
making war. You have done splendid work with

your *llaneros*. I know how much I can rely on you.'

'General, the cause of liberty has been the only guide of all my actions. I am happy if you can think me useful, for your devotion to Venezuela is the glory of us all. I am no scholar, my family was too poor to have me educated, but I hope to make up for my ignorance by my contempt for danger. I should like to show you on the spot that, when it comes to fighting for the Republic, my lancers and I fear nothing.'

'I am sure of it, Paez, and I shall often enough have need of your valour. The Apure is a wide river and my flotilla takes a long time to come. Ah! If I had only those three enemy gunboats which are moored on the other bank, I could attack the Spaniards this very evening.'

'Don't worry about that, General, you shall see what my guard can do.'

And Paez called the fifty *llaneros* whom he had chosen for their bravery:

'Friends, you see those boats, we must take them or die. Forward.'

And he urged his horse into the river, at this point a kilometre wide, and full of crocodiles. His men followed him, and, swimming furiously, took possession of the boats, amidst the joyful shouts of all the Venezuelan army who witnessed this feat of arms.

That night Bolivar attacked Morillo and beat him soundly at La Hogaza.

Bolivar established his headquarters in a farm

called *El Rincon de los Toros* (Bull Corner). A Spanish detachment, guided by a deserter, tried to surprise
the Liberator during the night. As they knew the pass-
word a dozen soldiers penetrated as far as the house,
where they met Colonel Santander, who, deceived by
the darkness, asked them who they wanted. 'We
want the Commander-in-Chief.' Santander called
out, but Bolivar, awakened by the noise, sprang onto
his horse to see what was happening. The Spaniards
fired and wounded the horse; Bolivar hastened to the
head of his men, and counter-attacked, killing the
enemy colonel. But the army, seeing the Liberator's
horse riderless and covered with blood, were panic-
stricken, and Bolivar had great difficulty in rallying
them to the fight, in the middle of such thick darkness
that men shot without knowing at whom they were
firing.

On February 26, 1818, at Cumaná, Mariño, whose
disposition was not bad, but who was of headstrong
character, made public apology to the Government
of Angostura. He even addressed his troops and ordered them thenceforward to obey the orders of the
Liberator, whose most faithful subject he intended
to become.

Bolivar was prostrated by a dangerous fever and
obliged to defer his expedition against New Granada.
His doctor ordered him to rest before resuming the
campaign, and forbade him to leave his room for a
fortnight.

XXX

RETURNING to Angostura, Bolivar profited by his forced inaction to write to his cousin Fanny, whom he had not forgotten and whom from time to time he kept informed of his successes and vexations. He drew up a 'Proclamation to the Old World,' on which he had often meditated.

Interpreter of the Will of the Nation, the Venezuelan Government asserts before all the world:

1. That the Republic of Venezuela, by divine right and the right of man, has separated herself from Spain, and constituted herself a sovereign, free and independent State.

2. That Spain has no more right to exercise sovereignty than has Europe to attempt to subject us to that Power.

3. That the Republic has not sought and will never seek to be incorporated with Spain.

4. That she has not asked for the intervention of the Great Powers to make peace with Spain.

5. That she will never treat with Spain save as Power to Power, in peace as in war, as all nations treat with one another.

6. That she desires the intervention of foreign States merely that they may urge Spain to sign a treaty of peace and friendship with the Venezuelan

nation, and to recognize Venezuela as an independent Republic.

7. That Venezuela has been fighting for her rights since the 19th of April, 1810, that she has shed the blood of almost all her sons, that she has sacrificed her wealth and all things dear and sacred to the heart of man. If Spain or Europe or the whole world persist in trying to thrust her again beneath a hateful yoke, the people of Venezuela are ready to bury themselves in her ruins rather than relinquish any of the rights with which Providence has endowed them.

XXXI

On the 21st of January, 1819, the arrival of two ships flying the British flag was signalled at Angostura. The Perseverance and the Tartar brought a body of English volunteers, under a colonel, who came to put themselves at Bolivar's disposal, to fight at his side.

All the men were well armed; some of them came from military colleges and presented themselves to Bolivar with letters of recommendation from their fathers who had known the Liberator in London in 1810. Bolivar formed a separate regiment of these new recruits, taking on to his general staff several of the officers, among them the Irishman O'Leary, who became his aide-de-camp and noted down the smallest events of every day.

In spite of the unfavourable season Bolivar sent Colonel Santander, a better lawyer than soldier, to New Granada with the task of uniting the guerrilla bands in the south and of spreading everywhere such rumours as were likely to raise the courage of the Granadans. He was to say that Morillo was beaten, twenty thousand Spaniards killed, that the republican army was sweeping all before it, and that Spain, brought to a standstill by the expenses and the excessive losses which this war had cost her, asked no more than to make peace, and that South America's day was dawning at last. The Granadan soldiers should join the Venezuelans and presently the liberated soil would no longer bear a single Spaniard.

Bolivar laid down his office of Dictator, on the grounds that he could not attend at the same time to both civil and military affairs. He demanded the election of a President and a Vice-President.

He was unanimously elected President of the Republic. Zea, the Vice-President, was to attend to the administration in the absence of the Liberator.

Morillo crossed the Apure with all his army.

Paez pursued him, avoiding a pitched battle, but never ceasing to harry the Spaniards, to lay traps for them, scatter them, kill as many as possible, and to spare not one who crossed his path.

At Queseras del Medio, with a hundred and fifty *llaneros*, Paez appeared before the Spanish bridge, and, making an abrupt half-turn, feigned flight. The Spaniards rushed after him. When Paez had reached the main body of his cavalry, who were waiting, he gave the word and faced about, every man with a lance presented. The Spaniards, who could make nothing of this sudden change of tactics and had not even time to put themselves in a defensive position, were trampled underfoot by the hurricane of *llaneros*. The victory cost only six men wounded. The Spaniards left behind them more than four hundred dead.

It was the rainy season: all the plains were flooded. Morillo had taken shelter in an entrenched camp, which he did not intend to leave for two or three months.

Bolivar assembled a council of war and pointed out the necessity of attacking New Granada at a time of year when nobody could expect it. Santander had returned very well satisfied with his mission; the Liberator was everywhere impatiently awaited.

On May 26th, Bolivar took the road at the head of thirteen hundred foot and eight hundred horse. He did not at first let them know what direction he was taking, for he knew what fear lowland peasants feel in a mountainous country.

The army frequently marched up to the waist in water; gradually they built themselves rafts, made from trees bound together with creepers, and poled their way forward.

On the 12th of June, they reached the Andes.

The crossing of these mountains was to be still more toilsome than that which Bolivar had accomplished in coming from Magdalena. Many of the *llaneros* had never seen the Cordilleras, some had not even heard of their existence. Their astonishment grew increasingly great, for the mountains became higher and higher. Men began to desert, horses slipped and mules staggered beneath their loads. A cold rain fell without intermission; men died of dysentery for lack of attention. Bolivar, wonderful in his confidence and serenity, talked to his soldiers of the glorious country which lay before them; he pictured its riches and the welcome of its inhabitants. In his presence nobody dared to complain.

A Spanish post was taken on June 27th. So little did the garrison suspect an attack that the patriots got the better of them directly. This success was excellent for their morale.

Bolivar chose the most difficult roads, sure to find them less well guarded. Not a house, not a light, impossible to kindle a fire in the persistent rain, icy cold, and in these seemingly insurmountable difficulties a half-naked army fresh from the scorching plains of Guiana.

Many women had followed their husbands; one night during a halt one of them was seized with the pains of childbirth. They rigged up a tent for her. Bolivar went to see the sick woman and congratulated her on her endurance. Next day the force resumed its march and the woman followed with her baby in her arms.

Bolivar talked ceaselessly to his men, foretold their victory and the coming end of all their sufferings — only three days more, only two. . . . Not for an instant did he consider his own fatigue. He ate the same food as his troopers, raw meat barely salted.

Bolivar's arrival in New Granada had a prodigious effect. The Spaniards could not understand how the Cordilleras had been crossed; the inhabitants, weary of the enemy yoke, brought munitions and food to the Venezuelans. After such privations nothing more was needed to put them in good heart. Hundreds of peasants joined the Liberator.

On the 3d of August Bolivar was informed of the

appearance of the Spanish General Barreyro; by clever manœuvring he drew him towards the bridge at Boyaca. Leaving Santander to hold him in check, he set off immediately to cut the road to Bogotá, and ordered Anzoategui to attack with his cavalry. The stratagem succeeded; after the two columns had gone into action, Bolivar returned on his tracks, and, taking the enemy in the rear, succeeded in routing him.

Sixteen hundred men were taken prisoner, among whom were all the generals and colonels of this Spanish army.

Bolivar noticed Captain Vinoni among the prisoners. He called him out of the ranks, and looking fixedly at him he said:

'Have you forgotten your ignoble treachery at Puerto Cabello? You do not even deserve a soldier's death.'

And he had him hanged then and there.

On August 10th, Bolivar made his entry into Santa Fé de Bogotá, which the Spaniards had abandoned in the most complete disorder. He confiscated all the enemy property, and found in the Viceroy's treasury more than six hundred thousand piastres. With this money he was able at last to settle affairs and to distribute some rewards to his victorious soldiers.

XXXII

With their arms full of provisions and of gifts, the inhabitants of the towns flocked to meet the Liberator.

Triumphal arches marked Bolivar's progress. People walked for leagues in order to touch his garments. The soldiers, who had forgotten the fatigues of their crossing of the Andes and who at last realized their leader's genius, were ready thenceforward for any trial that he chose to suggest to them.

Everywhere Bolivar spoke of the good relations between New Granada and Venezuela; the nations were brothers; the Venezuelans were doing no more than pay their debts, for President Torres on his side had not hesitated to attempt the deliverance of the province of Caracas. Out of the wealth abandoned by the Spaniards, the Liberator allotted pensions to all the victims of enemy atrocities and to the widows of his soldiers. Santander was appointed Vice-President of Bogotá.

Bolivar continued his victorious march, but the news which he received from Angostura compelled him to return to that town after having handed over his army to Anzoategui.

There was neither more nor less than conspiracy at Angostura. The Congress were disturbed by what they termed Bolivar's boundless ambition; they blamed him for having abandoned Venezuela to seek fame in distant countries; they even called it treason for him to have defeated the enemy outside their own frontiers.

With a small escort Bolivar traversed fifteen hundred kilometres; he was in a hurry to clear the matter up and to know what was required of him. He arrived, and without an instant's rest appeared before the Congress and announced:

'Here I am. The enemy is beaten everywhere, the whole province of Santa Fé is occupied by our troops; I am driving the Spaniards into their last entrenchments, all the people of Granada have risen on our side; victory smiles on us, there will soon be not a single royalist in Tierra Firme. Is not that enough for you? If any one here has any criticisms to make, let him stand up, let him tell me with what the country can reproach me!'

In the town, meanwhile, Bolivar's horsemen had been relating the prodigious success of their leader; a crowd had gathered in front of the Hall of Congress demanding the Liberator and cheering his name. No longer did a single deputy find a word to say against his conduct. When Bolivar showed himself at the window, he was received with shouts of joy. They wanted to carry him in triumph. Bolivar turned towards the men who a few minutes earlier had been minded to try him for treason.

'Now,' said he, 'to work.'

The Congress drafted the basis of the Colombian Republic, thus composed:

Venezuela: President, Bolivar.
New Granada: Vice-President, Santander.
Ecuador: Vice-President, Roscio.

Zea was to sail as soon as possible for Europe, his mission being to get the State recognized by the Great Powers and to negotiate a loan in England.

José de Sucre, an upright young colonel, the only man on whose honesty Bolivar could really rely, was ordered to go to the West Indies with a very large sum of money brought by Bolivar, and to buy arms there.

The Liberator at once returned to Bogotá. General Anzoategui had just died as the result of a wound. Bolivar was informed of the execution of the captive Spanish Commander Barreyro. He demanded an explanation from Santander, for Barreyro was a general who had always fought fairly. Santander replied that he had been forced to this extremity by the wishes of the people, who were enraged at measures taken by the enemy, and especially by the death of a patriot girl of eighteen who had been shot a short time before at Cartagena by order of the Viceroy Semano. The Bogotans had not forgotten the gallant death of Pola Salavarrieta, who had refused to hand over to the Spaniards documents which her fiancé had carried. The people of Granada demanded vengeance, which Santander declared that he could not refuse, regretting at the same time that it should have fallen on Barreyro, whose end had been touching. The Spanish general, who had secretly loved a republican woman, begged the commander of the firing party to convey a portrait to her, with a letter in which he expressed his regret at having fought against the patriots and the hope that at least his death would serve to hasten peace.

XXXIII

MORILLO wrote to Ferdinand VII to report on the critical situation in which he found himself. His troops had suffered considerable losses, all the reënforcements which he might have expected from Porto Rico and Peru had been used up; he had no more fighting men but the garrisons in the north of New Granada, inadequate against so strong an adversary as Bolivar, whose army swelled from day to day, and whose soldiers, knowing the country and supported by its inhabitants, were increasingly to be feared.

A formidable expedition was in preparation in the south of Andalusia. This war was dragging out, and Spain began to weary of the continual demands of her generals. The colonies must be subdued at all costs.

Happily for them a military rising led by Captain Riego forced Ferdinand VII to restore the Constitution of Cadiz, which the King had quietly suppressed when he regained his throne. Difficulties sprang up on every side, and little by little the expeditionary force melted away. There was a hope that the restoration of the Constitution would be enough to satisfy the American republicans. They, on the contrary, saw in the abdication of royal authority but a result of their demands; since the central government had given way on one point, it might give way on others. The last defenders of Spanish rule came over to the republican side.

Morillo, who was well aware of his danger, made proposals to Bolivar for an amnesty. Bolivar replied that he represented not merely Venezuela, but the whole of South America, and, as Morillo seemed prepared to continue the war, he let him know that the people of Colombia did not intend to have terms dictated to them, but were determined to free themselves entirely from the royal yoke.

On November 25th, at Trujillo, Morillo consented to sign a treaty for 'Regularization of the War.' It was now no longer a question of punishing rebellious subjects, but of fighting against a nation.

Bolivar wrote to the Congress informing them of the proposals for submission to Spain which he had received from Morillo:

'Shall we forget the hundreds of victories we have won from the enemy, shall we disown our glory, our rights and the heroism of our soldiers? Colombia will never allow herself to be governed by that ancient Spain which is the shame of Europe.'

The Treaty of Trujillo was signed in the very same house where Bolivar had declared war to the death.

Morillo sent General Correa, Don Juan Rodriguez del Toro, and Linares to ask for an armistice. Since the Spaniards had admitted the regularization of the war, Bolivar ordered Sucre, whom he had made a general, Colonel Briceño Mendez, and Lieutenant-Colonel Perez to negotiate with Morillo's messengers.

An armistice for six months was signed.

Morillo, having made known his wish to discuss the situation with Bolivar, the two men arranged a rendezvous on November 27th at the village of Santa Ana.

Morillo arrived first, followed by his staff and a squadron of hussars. Bolivar's aide-de-camp, the Irishman O'Leary, had gone to meet him.

'Do you notice among my suite,' Morillo asked him, 'any officers whom the President would not care to meet, or for whom he has a particular dislike? Does he intend to come with a stronger escort than mine?'

'I do not see any officers that the President especially hates,' replied O'Leary; 'and in any case the President will be accompanied by only about ten of his men.'

'In that case he shows himself more generous than I am,' said Morillo, and dismissed the whole of his Hussars.

The two commanders dismounted, and with one impulse shook hands. The Spaniard wore full uniform and had put on all his decorations; the Venezuelan had only an old blue overcoat and a police cap.

A modest meal was prepared in the most comfortable house of the village. The two rivals sat down face to face and talked the whole day, complimenting one another on their courage and tenacity. They spent the night beneath the same roof, in revenge, so they said, for all the bad nights that they had deliberately given each other.

In the morning when Morillo came down, he found

Bolivar already up and waiting to take coffee with him.

'I suggest,' said Morillo, 'that a monument should be put up in this village to commemorate the perfect courtesy of our relations and to recall to future generations the fact that personal malice and national hatred should be forgotten in the presence of sincerity and loyalty.'

The officers fetched a heavy stone, which was placed in front of the house.

Morillo, conqueror of Napoleon and the greatest general of Spain, wrung the hand of the Creole who had just vanquished him.

The two men were never to meet again.

XXXIV

MORILLO was recalled to Spain and the armistice found itself undermined from both sides.

On the 28th of January, the town of Maracaibo declared itself for the Republic and revolted against the Spanish garrison. Exchanges of notes, mutual threats, and accusations of bad faith in regard to the clauses of the treaty rendered the peace more and more doubtful.

With one accord Bolivar and la Torre, who had replaced Morillo, decided to resume hostilities from the date of April 28th.

Bolivar ordered his soldiers to respect the Treaty of Trujillo and threatened with death any one who murdered a prisoner or committed an atrocity.

After some unimportant skirmishing, the two armies met at Carabobo. The Spaniards were the better placed and their position seemed impregnable. Paez took a briar-choked path at the bottom of a ravine in order to turn the enemy's right flank, but so narrow was the way that his horsemen were obliged to advance in Indian file, and when they reached the end they came upon four of the strongest Spanish battalions, who shot them down at leisure. The magnificent stand of the British Legion, whose men, kneeling on one knee, fired without ceasing, at last allowed the *llaneros* to re-form. Paez's bodyguard and General Herras's infantry then came into action, and, attacking the royalists from several points at once, ended by driving them out of their entrenchments.

Only four hundred Spaniards out of six thousand returned to Puerto Cabello; they were hunted to the very gates. This victory destroyed the finest royalist army, but it cost the republicans dear, for several of their field officers and many officers of the British Legion had been killed.

Bolivar promoted Paez to the rank of Commander-in-Chief.

The Congress of Colombia met in extraordinary assembly at Rosario de Cucuta. It decreed a triumphal entry for Bolivar and his soldiers. The anniversary of the victory of Carabobo was to be a holiday every year throughout the country. Bolivar's portrait was hung in the Assembly Room with the inscription:

SIMON BOLIVAR
THE LIBERATOR OF COLOMBIA

Almost the whole of Venezuela had now been freed. Bolivar returned to Caracas, where he found his house just as he had left it; in their retreat the enemy had not had time to pillage it. But the Liberator had no leisure to delay over his own affairs. He heard almost simultaneously of a brilliant victory by Sucre, in the south of Yaguachi; and then a defeat of the same commander at Guachi.

Bolivar left once more for Bogotá and took the

head of his troops for a march on Quito. He defeated the Spaniards at Bombona after a deadly battle; but Sucre had not waited for him; victorious at Pichincha, he had entered Quito on May 22, 1822.

Ecuador in its turn was liberated. On July 31st a popular assembly at Guayaquil decreed its union with Colombia.

It is possible to get some idea of Bolivar's almost incredible activity by following upon a map his comings and goings in a country as large as Europe.

The roads were non-existent, the mountains often insurmountable, the rivers wide and infested by alligators, the forests thick and full of wild beasts. Nothing could stop the Liberator. He had an army which never exceeded seven or eight thousand men. Victorious in the north, he would set off for the south and fight fresh battles. Never a day's rest. Moreover, he did not like to keep his soldiers too long without a fight. Many deserted during the lulls, and Bolivar endeavoured to leave them not even time to think. He preferred to think for them.

XXXV

At Guayaquil, Bolivar met José de San Martín. The general from La Plata had just freed Chile and part of Peru. He had ridden into Lima with his *gauchos*, horsemen as formidable as the *llaneros*. He came to Guayaquil on purpose to make Bolivar's acquaintance.

The struggle of these two men against the Spanish yoke had greatly attracted them to one another, but for the last two years their attempts to meet had been in vain.

San Martín, worn out by these wars, handed on to Bolivar the task of completing the victory. He had only one wish, to return to France and finish his days there. Bolivar accepted the charge and vowed to the Argentine that he would leave no part of South America in Spanish hands.

Victorious on the battle-field, Bolivar made proclamations to his fellow-citizens:

'Your glorious fatherland is free at last, the victories of Bombona and Pichincha have completed the work which your heroism began. From Orinoco to the Andes of Peru the army of liberty has marched from success to success. Only one town still holds out, but not for long.

'South Colombians! The blood of your brothers

has redeemed you from the horrors of war. It has won for you enjoyment of the sacred rights of Justice and Equality.

'The laws of Colombia consecrate the union between social privileges and natural rights. The Constitution of Colombia is the pattern of a government, representative, republican, and strong. You cannot hope to find a better the whole world over.'

But while Bolivar was winning battles, the Congress was revising his schemes for a constitution and little by little perverting them completely.

Bolivar had insisted on an hereditary senate, for he knew that an absolute democracy was much more dangerous than the worst despotism. Democracy needed a bridle, and, since it was necessary, what matter if this bridle were an institution frankly aristocratic?

Bolivar mistrusted his fellow-citizens and did not blind himself to the fact. Paez punished his *llaneros* by fighting them; it was an excellent method in time of war and with a general like Paez, but how was one to govern men so utterly lacking in moral feelings, who had fought first for the royalists, then for the republicans, simply according to the inclination of their leaders? The Indians and the half-castes were more peaceable and above all more honest, but few of them could read. Under no circumstances did Bolivar wish for universal suffrage. Draconian laws were useful while waiting for those of Solon, and the Colombian nation was not yet steady enough to receive very advanced institutions.

To embrace so scattered a republic as that of Colombia, an absolute government was required, strong enough to resist the difficulties inherent in such a country. Now the Congress feared that a dictatorial President would act simply at his own will. Every one wished to command, to satisfy his own ambition, and this was the beginning of that anarchy which Bolivar was to try to exorcise for the next nine years.

First and foremost the Congress decided that the senators should be elected for eight years only; that domestic servants and day labourers alone should be deprived of votes. The dictatorial powers of Bolivar were left to him for the duration of the war and no longer.

It was understood that these laws were, so to speak, provisional only. The Congress undertook to revise them in 1840, and then to consider the Constitution of Bolivar. But there were twenty years certain of demagogue rule, of which the members of the Government intended to make the most.

XXXVI

THE Inca race had not entirely forgotten the atrocities and the perfidy of Pizarro when he conquered Peru at the beginning of the sixteenth century. Cuzco, a very ancient town, was founded, says tradition, by the hero Manco Ccapac, come from the hot countries with a great rod of gold in his hand, the symbol of his power. Manco Ccapac halted one day with his sister Mama Occlo on a mountain from which they could see a circular plain surrounded by hills. They decided to settle there and gave it the name of Cuzco, which means 'navel of the world.' Now tradition had it, even in 1822, that an underground lake existed beneath the cathedral and that the water of this lake began to boil every year on the anniversary of Pizarro's arrival. No threat was sufficient to prevent the Incas from making obeisance as they passed the place.

The most serious insurrection against the Spanish authority was that of the cacique Tupac Amaru at the end of the eighteenth century.

At this time the governors of certain districts had the exclusive right of supplying the natives with the most necessary goods. This privilege led very rapidly to abuses; the prices demanded by the Spaniards were so excessive that the inhabitants of the country lived in most terrible destitution. A cacique called José Gabriel Condorcanque took the name of Tupac

Amaru, the last Inca king, killed by the invaders. The cacique sent his two brothers to the court of Charles III to ask the King to revise the oppressive laws of Peru. The two messengers died in Madrid in so mysterious a way, and the royal authorities looked on Tupac Amaru with such animosity, that he was obliged to flee. He put himself at the head of the populace of those parts and revolted openly against the Viceroy. After winning some victories and hanging with his own hands the Corregidor of Tinta, he was betrayed and delivered to the Spaniards by the cacique Pumacahua. Tupac Amaru was dragged to torture, with his wife, his children, and all his relations that could be laid hands on. They were cut to pieces while still living, by order of the Viceroy. People who were present at this frightful execution could never to the end of their days forget its terrible cruelty. As for the traitor Pumacahua, the Spaniards found it simpler to cut off his head than to reward him.

After this horrible repression, it seemed that all danger of rebellion was averted.

Peru was the last country to revolt, and it did not do so till after the liberation of Colombia by Bolivar.

The Argentine General San Martín had entered Lima on July 12, 1821, and independence had been at once proclaimed. San Martín took the title of Protector, and as long as he remained in the town no disorder showed itself. Extremely firm, he allowed no politician to influence him; but tired out by the swift and dangerous campaigns that he had led, he sent in his resignation. It was at this stage that he met Bolivar.

When he had departed, the most complete anarchy showed itself in the Government. The Spaniards made the most of it, and, having had time to reorganize their army, they resumed the offensive. To resist them the Peruvian Government set up a triumvirate without much authority. Poverty reigned among the lower classes, but the Congress cared for that as little as it disturbed itself over the Spanish advance; only political questions interested it. It refused Bolivar's help. The Peruvian troops overthrew the Directorate; a President was elected and appealed to San Martín, who answered him by a contemptuous letter. The President was replaced by another, Torre Tagle, who, with the connivance of an untrustworthy Minister, made overtures to Spain. His treachery seemed natural in that faithless Government.

Then San Martín wrote to Bolivar:

'Protect this unhappy nation; you alone, Bolivar, are capable of delivering it from its madness. God Himself would be powerless, but I know you, and I have confidence in you.'

The Spaniards seized Lima, and then only was Bolivar implored to intervene.

The wife of an English doctor at Quito called James Thorne had left her husband to follow Bolivar, whom she loved. She had resumed her maiden name, Manuela Saenz, and become the Liberator's mistress.

At the time when Peru's despairing appeal reached Bolivar, he was living in Bogotá with this woman. At times she frightened him by her energy; before her he had only loved poor Teresa and then Fanny, both of them sweet and sentimental; the others had merely passed through his tempestuous life. Manuela was tall, well made, and strong. She said to her lover:

'You are going away to begin the war again in the south. I cannot bear to leave you; I shall go with you.'

She had a red jacket made for herself with gold facings, and wide white linen trousers; she rode astride on a thoroughbred horse and carried in her belt a sword and pistols. Bolivar took her with him.

His army was small in numbers, but composed entirely of veterans in whom he had every confidence. Sucre, who had become one of his greatest generals, and whose admirable qualities he knew, he sent on in advance. He defeated the Spanish General Cauterac, and Bolivar entered Lima without striking a blow. But the situation was grave. It was known that the Spaniards were engaged in reconstituting a corps of more than seventy thousand men. There was no more money in the Treasury.

Bolivar was appointed Dictator of Peru, and in Lima all was feasting and joy. Bolivar was welcomed as a god; he was fawned upon, and for the first time in his life he allowed himself to be worshipped; he felt the need of happiness at last. As he strolled with his mistress through streets bordered with flowering gardens, he was sure of victory; no matter that the Spaniards were preparing for an attack, he was not afraid of them, he had beaten them a thousand times already and had no fear that they would ever defeat him.

Lima was the most beautiful town in South America. Its people maintained that the Eternal Father had had a window contrived in the floor of Paradise so that He could look at it for ever. Wonderful monuments, shady parks, fountains, statues. At every step Bolivar put up clouds of swallows. A warm climate, freshened from time to time by light breezes, conduced to luxurious habits. Bolivar danced every night amidst all the nobility and the dazzling women, who adored him. He gave rein at last to the passion for dancing which the most deadly battle had never destroyed in him.

But Bolivar was not content to worship pleasure alone. Accompanied by Manuela, as indefatigable as himself, he inspected the mines, founded a university and schools, and watched over the minutest details of the administration.

The most superhuman vigour has its limits, and, returning one day to the house, whose every window-sill was crowded with flowers and cages of birds, Bolivar suddenly realized that he was exceedingly tired.

His doctor examined him carefully, ordered the most absolute rest, made him promise to leave that unhealthy town, and advised him to retire into the

SIMON BOLIVAR
From an English engraving

country far from all noise and distraction, military or political. Bolivar was obliged to yield. He himself felt that he had reached his limit.

Before he went he glanced back at the house he was quitting, and could not restrain a smile at an old one-eyed Indian in the courtyard who was training some dogs to drill.

XXXVII

Disagreements inevitably occur between politicians and generals. Bolivar was accused of having reserved the best posts for his favourite lieutenants. The first to suffer from these attacks was the Vice-President of Colombia, General Antonio Nariño, one of the finest figures of the epoch. Nariño was impeached before the Congress of Rosario de Cucuta on a charge of abuse of power and treason. He met it by a simple story of his life.

Born at Santa Fé de Bogotá on April 14, 1765, of a noble family, he received a very careful education and became the most brilliant pupil at Saint Bartholomew's College.

He was appointed Treasurer of Tithes by the Vice-Chancellor, and utilized the spare time which his post afforded for the completion of his studies. Being fairly rich, he was able to form a library of about six thousand volumes. He entertained all the youth of Bogotá at his house, in a room where the portrait of Franklin held the place of honour. They read aloud from French and English authors and translated Greek and Latin ones; by degrees they began to talk politics and to take an interest in the French Revolution.

One night, when Nariño was working at home, an officer brought him a book which he had found by chance and which might perhaps be of some rarity:

It was the 'Histoire de l'Assemblée Constituante,' by Salart de Montjoie.

Nariño thanked the officer and began to read the three volumes. He found there the text of the 'Declaration of the Rights of Man.' Wild with enthusiasm, he translated this manifesto into Spanish, bought a little printing-office and struck off a great many copies which he distributed here and there. The influence of these leaflets was considerable; the Captain-General was alarmed, and gave orders to withdraw them from circulation; Nariño and several of his friends were arrested. Nariño was condemned to ten years in the hulks, his family was proscribed, and all his goods sold.

But when he arrived at Cadiz, he shook off his two guards and escaped, borrowed money from some friends of his father who lived in the town, slipped across into France, and from there to England.

In London he became acquainted with Miranda and Bolivar, and decided to go back to his own country. After a thousand difficulties he reached Santa Fé, where, denounced by the servants, he was arrested and sent to Madrid. He remained there for more than ten years in the military prison. With unheard-of perseverance he watched his moment to escape. He got away at last, and lived the life of a beggar, hunted by the police, hiding during the daytime in a wood, where he relieved a traveller of his valise, made friends with some smugglers, and departed once again for Santa Fé. There be behaved with greater prudence, but, once more betrayed, he was condemned to the Spanish galleys. On the Magdalena he jumped into the river and fled. He was recaptured, dying of hunger, by the local authorities, who locked him up in the cells at Cartagena des Indes; they put fetters on his feet and circled his waist with six metres of heavy chains.

Thanks to the rising of 1810, he was set free and was able to play a part in the Revolution. Editor of an advanced journal, then a general, after a blaze of glory he was all at once detested. Infamous lies were circulated about him. One day when he returned to his house, he found a man sent there to murder him.

'Here are the keys of the house,' said Nariño to him, 'so it will be easy for you to go when you have killed me.'

The man was disarmed by such coolness. He flung himself at the general's feet.

'Very well, then, sit down for a minute and let us talk about our country.'

In April, 1814, at the head of a small detachment, a last remnant of the patriot armies, he came across the Spanish General Aymerich. The enemy was on the farther side of the Juanambu, a wild torrent. In the night Nariño sent several men across to the other bank to stretch cables so that the soldiers could be brought over in baskets. The Spaniards discovered the stratagem and cut the cables. In order not to abandon the party on the opposite shore, Nariño ordered his tallest men to cross the torrents carrying the shorter ones on their shoulders. These latter fired as they advanced and the enemy were driven from their position. But Nariño was in a hostile country and the greater part of his soldiers deserted.

Soon left alone, he tried to conceal himself in the woods, but he was made prisoner and sent to Popayran, a town faithful to the royalists. He found an infuriated populace who threatened and insulted him. Pushing aside the guards who protected him from the rage of the mob, he stepped forward, arms folded, crying: 'Behold me. I am General Nariño.'

His voice was so resolute and scornful that the people dropped the stones they had been meaning to throw at him.

Sent first to the dungeons of Quito, then to Callao, fettered on a boat which took ten months to reach Spain, he was put at last into solitary confinement at Madrid, naked, almost starved, and ill-treated by his jailers. Nothing could break him. In 1820, the military insurrection of Captain Puega, whose object was the reëstablishment of the Constitution, enabled him to get free. Without hesitation he set off for Gibraltar. Captain Diego commissioned him to announce the confirmation of the Constitution in New Granada. Nariño took advantage of this unhoped-for mission to sail for his own country. Once more a general, after many and various services he was appointed Vice-President of Colombia.

Before the Congress at Cucuta he overwhelmed his

accusers by the history of his sufferings. He was acquitted; but a few weeks later, abandoned by every one and worn out by so much privation and ill treatment, he died miserably, bequeathing to the Republic what little remained to him, and speaking these last words:

'I loved my country. History will show with what love.'

He was the first victim to party jealousy.

XXXVIII

IN the little country house whither he had retired with Manuela, Bolivar experienced the deepest grief at the news of this death. He too had loved his country and he loved it still, but he was more and more sickened by the lack of honesty in his countrymen. He knew that they feared him and that in his presence anarchy dared not fully reveal itself; but after his death what a deluge, what disorder! Every one would wish to rule and Colombia would fall into the hands of any foreign Power.

For too long Bolivar had despised illness; even had it not been so, his anxieties had been too many to allow him to take care of himself. Now came the consequence of all that fatigue. San Martín was tired out and his people were unstable, Bolivar had not even the right to be tired of his: his departure would be the signal for terrible disasters. José de Sucre might perhaps be able to finish the work of liberation, but Sucre was too straightforward, too honest to withstand the intrigues of the lowest sort of politicians. At the same time, in a moment of depression, Bolivar wrote to him:

MY DEAR JOSÉ: To make an end of the war I am ready to fight one battle against the Spaniards and no more. I feel that I have come to the end of my tether, an old man in spite of my forty years, and I have nothing more to hope from Fate. I am the dotard always worrying over his money. Everything gives me occasion for fears and alarms, and each instant I expect to lose my reputation, the only reward of all my sacrifices. The same thing will happen to you, but you are very young, a magnificent future lies before you. If I could but find myself in your shoes and have nothing to fear from Fortune, I should at least have hopes and desires to make me forget my cares.

Manuela's devotion was sublime, she never left the Liberator's bedside, and warded off everything that might be a cause of trouble or excitement. When possible she suppressed the news, which was bad.

Peru was rent with civil war. The Viceroy Laserna had at last succeeded in reorganizing an army of twenty-five thousand men, all the best troops that Spain possessed on the American continent. Not raw recruits; nothing but seasoned soldiers who were accustomed to the country and who were in haste to take a resounding revenge.

The Congress of Bogotá was greatly agitated by the danger and realized that the Peruvian troops were incapable of defending Lima. They decided to make yet one more appeal to Bolivar.

A Minister, reputed to be his friend, was sent to beg him to return to power and withdraw his resignation. Bolivar was ill, feverish, he listened to the messenger sitting up in bed.

'What do you mean to do?' asked his household.

'Conquer, of course,' replied Bolivar.

He got up, made his preparations to depart, and next day set out for the coast, for he had no army. He enlisted new troops. Manuela wore her red jacket. Bolivar had made her the present of a dagger with a carved handle, which never left her.

Thanks to his experience, the Liberator got together a sound army; he was obeyed by his officers, who saw in him still the miraculous conqueror. But Bolivar had not his former confidence. The people no longer helped him; the Congress refused the sums of money that he demanded.

On August 6th, Bolivar learned that the Spanish General Cauterac was in the neighbourhood. He wanted to make the most of this chance, and started at once to fight with him. He met him at Junin, and in his hurry to make an end of things he charged in person at the head of his cavalry, as in the old guerrilla days. The Spaniards were routed, but Bolivar was not satisfied; he had not destroyed all the enemy and the war was not finished. Ah, how he would have liked to fight a second battle that very day!

The Congress knew that there was only one man with influence: Bolivar. If his prestige were to be tarnished in any way whatever, all was over with the Republic.

Bolivar was sure to conquer, but the Fates might be against him, and if he were defeated, even slightly, nothing would hold the people. A diminution of his fame must be avoided above all things. If it were another general who was beaten, Bolivar's glory would remain untouched and there would be still time to let him intervene. The stake was too high to be risked on a single card.

In an excited council of war where all these reasons were brought forward, Bolivar consented to relinquish the supreme command to General Sucre. Bolivar would decide on the plan of campaign, on the whole course to be followed, but his name would be replaced by another's.

On the 9th of December, 1824, after very brilliant operations, Sucre found himself opposed by the Viceroy Laserna on the plain of Ayacucho. Sucre had only six thousand men, the Spaniard had ten thousand, but nothing could daunt the vigour of the young general, who, rallying his troops ten times over and leaving not an instant's respite to an enemy who was yet his superior in numbers, succeeded in snatching the victory.

At a time when it would have been almost excusable for him to draw off his forces, which would have allowed the Spaniards to escape, Sucre in spite of his wounds decided to complete the victory. He pursued his adversary for miles; he gave no quarter. Bolivar had entrusted him with a task and he wished to acquit himself as thoroughly as possible.

By evening the Spanish army was destroyed.

The Viceroy, fifteen generals, sixteen colonels, sixty-eight lieutenant-colonels, two hundred officers, and two thousand men had laid down their arms and surrendered. All the artillery, the baggage train, and the munitions were in the hands of the conquerors.

Nothing remained of the last Spanish army in America.

When victory was no longer in doubt, Sucre wrote to Bolivar:

GENERAL: The war is over and the liberty of Peru assured. Nothing can give me greater happiness than the accomplishment of the mission with which you entrusted me. Our troops have showed admirable courage and I will give you the names of the officers and privates who seem to me to deserve the highest rewards. Farewell, General; forgive me if this letter is badly written, but it has at least the merit of containing the news of a great victory and of the liberation of Peru. The only reward I ask is to retain your friendship.

ANTONIO JOSÉ DE SUCRE

THE BATTLE FIELD OF AYACUCHO
December 9, 1824

Bolivar replied to this letter by coming immediately in person to congratulate the conqueror and by appointing him Grand Marshal of Ayacucho.

XXXIX

THE Peruvian Congress showed itself grateful for the victory of Ayacucho. Although Bolivar was not at the head of the troops, every one knew that the whole success of the campaign was due to him. They even for the moment forgot party hatred; thanks to his brilliant genius, a man had just succeeded in saving Peru and all the American colonies. He ought to be rewarded.

At Lima it was decided that:

An equestrian statue should be put up in the chief square.

A medal should be struck.

In the capital town of every Department a monument should commemorate the liberation of the country.

In the town halls, a portrait of Bolivar should hang in the Assembly Room in the place of honour.

Bolivar should for the rest of his life be entitled to the honours due to a President of the Republic.

He should also have a right to the title 'Father and Saviour of his Country.'

The Liberator should receive the sum of a million pesos for his own use.

A second million should be put at his disposal to
be divided among the soldiers.

Bolivar's popularity spread through the whole of
America. In the United States they put him on the
same level as Washington, and some even went so far
as to find him superior to the latter, for Washington
had not waged a fourteen-years war. In Europe the
papers extolled his genius; songs were made in his
honour, and folk remembered the young Venezuelan
traveller who had attained to universal fame. In
Spain they paid homage to his military and political
capacity, lacking which the New World would have
remained Castilian.

Bolivar had reached the highest pinnacle of his
glory.

He refused the money that was offered him and
accepted only that allotted to his men. To all his
honours he replied by extolling his generals and his
heroic soldiers. He asked that a sword whose hilt
was encrusted with precious stones should be sent to
Sucre, and that a special distinction should be reserved for all those who took part in the battle of
Ayacucho.

He besought the Congress to accept his resignation
as Dictator, an office which he had been obliged to
accept, but always against his will. Peru was saved;
there was no further need of an executive power, a
crying need in time of danger, but pointless now.

Envious folk tried to insinuate that Bolivar's resignation was not sincere, since he himself had said more than once that the exercise of power by a single individual had been the end of every democratic government.

But the Congress knew that, though victory over the Spaniards had been achieved, the social situation was a long way from stability and that it would take years to arrive at it. The Congress dreaded to see Bolivar retired before tranquillity was assured. No one could hold the country as the Liberator was able to do. Why abandon the Republic when she had more than ever need of a strong and wise hand to allow her to develop herself? The Congress owed it to itself to refuse this desertion. Bolivar had no right to resign.

Upper Peru constituted itself a province and asked permission to call itself Bolivia in homage to the Liberator. He agreed, but on condition that the capital should change its name of Chuquisaca for that of Sucre.

José de Sucre, Grand Marshal of Ayacucho, was elected President; he set to work at once and drew from Bolivar his inspiration to endow the country with republican institutions.

On the 23d January, 1826, the port of Callao, which was still in Spanish hands, was occupied by General Bartholomé Salom. Chile was definitely free.

The Spanish domination was only a memory.

XL

BOLIVAR, who always criticized his countrymen for their pretentiousness and above all for their ignorance, did his best to provide them with opportunities for instruction. In a liberated town his first care was to restore the schools; he himself drew up the syllabus, interviewed professors and sent for some from Europe. Colombia could not play her part as a Power until she possessed educated politicians. Formerly the rich families used to send their children to spend some years in Spain; that was no longer to be thought of, and it was in the country of their birth that the young Creoles must receive a model education.

At Cuzco, the old College of San Francisco de Borja was entirely remodelled, under the name of College of the Sun. Bolivar made a point of being present at the opening; he gave an address on the necessity of study. He had never forgotten what Humboldt had said to him about the remarkable gifts which that savant had observed in certain Americans. Bolivar wished that those gifts should have a chance to develop.

Many large towns were without a book-shop or even a printing-press. At Cuzco they printed journals, thanks to the press which the Viceroy Laserna had sent for from Lima to distribute manifestoes to the inhabitants, and had abandoned there. Bolivar was a great believer in the importance of journals; all his life he paid attention to the smallest newspaper articles and sought to use their wide influence.

But some one was about to come forward and meddle most disastrously with the educational projects of the Liberator.

One day it was noised about that Simon Rodriguez, who now called himself Samuel Robinson, had returned to Caracas after innumerable adventures all over the world. Bolivar had still a great respect for his old master, but this respect was mingled with affection for the tutor rather than for the doctrines of Rousseau, whose weakness Bolivar had been able to test.

At Bogotá, Santander made Rodriguez the director of a school. Rodriguez wished that men should learn from the great book of Nature and avoid the unhealthy and too numerous works of literature. He carried 'Emile' in his pocket and recommended manual labour to stabilize the brain. His dream was to carry some children, boys and girls, to a desert island while they were still quite young, and there to let them live upon a soil unstained by any crime.

A school in Bogotá was not enough for all the experiments that Rodriguez intended to try. He sought out Bolivar, and, in the tenderness of this interview after so many years of separation, secured from his former pupil a mission to go to Chuquisaca with a letter of recommendation to General Sucre, and there to found a university the most perfect in all South

America. Rodriguez was appointed Director of Public Instruction and Charities.

At Chuquisaca, Rodriguez went about with a French carpenter, a grotesque adventurer called Brutus, who was to teach the little Bolivians the manual trades prescribed by Rousseau. A magnificent hospital was established, but there were few patients. None the less Rodriguez appointed a director, a sub-director, and a numerous staff. He wrote incessantly to Bolivar asking for money, for all his schemes were bottomless gulfs; but the welfare of the people should be placed above such sordid considerations.

To teach anatomy Rodriguez walked naked among his pupils. That made a scandal. Parents who had sent their children to learn Latin and found them come back with a plane and some pincers, sent protests to Marshal Sucre.

Sucre, cold and sensible, had difficulty in putting up with the vagaries of the Director of Public Instruction. He sent a letter to Bolivar imploring him to take some steps about it.

'This Don Samuel Robinson of yours receives two thousand piastres a year for the hospital; he can shelter only fifteen poor souls and complains that he has not enough money. At the Asylum in Bogotá they have only fifteen hundred piastres, and they have a hundred patients. Obviously this is outrageous.

'As for the Frenchman Brutus, he does not even teach the children carpentering as had been arranged, and he gets five piastres a day, which he spends in the taverns. This has been going on for five months.

'Don Samuel Robinson is at loggerheads with all the officials here. At Cachabamba he has quarrelled with every one and treats them as brutes and ignoramuses. You see the result. But the most serious thing is that Don Samuel declares that within six months either he will have fallen or the religion of Jesus Christ will be turned out of Bolivia. Imagine the harm that such words may do.'

Rodriguez left this backward and undeserving town. He published a book: 'The Liberator of South America and his Companions in Arms Defended by a Friend of the Cause of Society.'

But Bolivar began to weary of these lunacies. Rodriguez departed, taking with him nothing but the manuscripts of his books. One night the house where he was lodging caught fire with all his manuscripts. Undismayed, the philosophic tutor resumed his wandering life, changing his trade every month, and talking about the happy future of the New World of which he believed himself to be the apostle.

XLI

BOLIVAR began to travel about the country, which was reverting quietly to peace, to agriculture, and to work. He went into the peasants' houses and entered into their schemes. He had had his own farms rebuilt and went sometimes to visit his farmers, for he had no longer time to deal with the cattle-raising himself.

He had often thought of making the ascent of Mount Chimborazo, which was at that time believed to be the highest spot on earth. With Manuela he set off for Quito, taking only a few devoted servants. From Quito he went to Chimborazo and climbed to more than sixty-eight hundred metres altitude. That night, carried away by the spirit of poetry, he wrote his celebrated 'Delirium,' where he found once more all the romantic side of his character, romanticism which wars and material cares had not been able to quench:

'Wrapped about in a rainbow, I came to the regions whence the river Orinoco bears its magnificent tribute to the god of waters. I had seen the unknown sources of the Amazon and I was fain to mount to the summit of the universe. I traced the footprints of La Condamine and Humboldt; my daring made me follow them; nothing could stop me. I reached the frozen heights. Until that day no human being had set foot upon the dazzling coronet with which Eternity has crowned the noble forehead of the Queen of the Andes.

'The rainbow, which lends its colours to my flag, has spanned the gulfs of Hell, crossed rivers and seas. Behold it on the Andes! What shall hinder me, even me, from reaching the snowy head of Chimborazo?

'Seized suddenly by a mysterious power, I leave behind the tracks of Humboldt and reach the eternal ice. Rapt by the genius which fills me, I stagger, my head strikes against the vault of Heaven. I am on the threshold of the Infinite. Delirium takes me, the God of Colombia possesses me. On a sudden, scythe in hand, appears before me Ancient Time, laden with the spoils of the ages:

'"I am the Father of the Centuries," he tells me; "I am stronger than Death; I behold the Past and the Future, and I grasp the Present in my hands. Whoever thou mayest be, dost thou fancy that thy universe is aught and that thou art lifted up because thou standest on an atom of creation?"

'Seized with a holy fear I answered him:

'"O Time, how shall a miserable mortal such as I behold thee and not swoon? I have surpassed the fortune of all humankind, since I have raised myself above them. The earth is beneath my feet, my arms reach to Heaven, I hear Hell seethe in the abyss, and I see the suns glitter around me."

'Then Time answers me:

'"Observe, learn, remember what thou hast seen;

tell it to thy fellows and unveil for them the secrets which the heavens have revealed to thee."

'For a long time I remain bereft of feeling, stretched upon this immense diamond which supports me. But the voice of Colombia draws me swiftly from my torpor. I awake, I rise up, I am once more a man . . .'

XLII

'WE grant the present letters of marque for a duration of three months, renewable. We authorize . . . to chase and capture all Spanish ships which he shall meet with on the high seas, to attack them in the rivers and in the roadsteads and harbours beneath our jurisdiction.

'We give express orders to . . . under the most severe penalties, that he shall uphold the honour and the good repute of the flag of Independence, shall molest none of the boats or vessels of friendly nations, but on the contrary shall come to their help in case of trouble. We make him responsible before the law for any abuse of power unjustly committed either by himself or by his crew.'

Supported by these licences, delighted to cloak their robberies beneath a flag and to plunder under the pretext of honest war, the pirates of the West Indies enlisted in the service of Colombia. In spite of increasing threats to his health, Bolivar relinquished none of his hatred of the Spaniards. He made plans to liberate Cuba and Porto Rico, which might be made into excellent naval bases; he went yet further and dreamed of harrying Spain herself. Sundry pirates went the length of attacking the Canary Isles, whose traffic was almost stopped, of entering the Mediterranean and of ravaging the coasts.

The Spanish Government was perturbed by these

feats, and since the republican cause was making alarming progress, above all in the ports, they feared every minute the arrival of a Creole squadron, come to avenge itself for centuries of slavery.

Spain had no more hope of reconquering her colonies; her internal dissensions were enough to occupy her soldiers. The authority of Ferdinand VII had been diminished by Riego's insurrection and was no longer respected as it once had been. A crowd of generals more or less suspected of the ambition to play dictator were watching for a moment of unrest. Ferdinand VII had only daughters, and felt that his succession was no easy question.

Bolivar at that time held an extraordinary aggregation of powers: he was at the same time head of Venezuela, New Granada, Peru, Ecuador, and Bolivia. He hoped to unite these states into a single one. Race, language, religion, habits — nothing was an obstacle to his design except the immensity of the territory. But it was just that immensity that demanded a single government. Bolivar saw, however, that this unity was not to be realized, but that, while yet remaining separate states, the different republics had such strong common interests that a mutual understanding ought to be achieved, from which each would benefit.

For a long time the Liberator had contemplated the setting up of a conference to which each country would be invited to send a representative to discuss the basis of an agreement.

The Isthmus of Panama seemed to be the perfect place for such a meeting.

In the month of June, 1826, Bolivar summoned all America to a congress. Chile, Patagonia, the Argentine, Brazil, Uruguay, and Paraguay neglected to answer the invitation.

The United States would consent to be present only if Bolivar would renounce his projects on Cuba and Porto Rico, which the Washington Government did not wish to see become independent republics, but preferred to seize from Spain at a later date. Neither would the United States hear any talk of the abolition of slavery; she wished to keep her distance from these states, the rebels of yesterday.

The conference was a lamentable failure.

At Washington the papers spread a hundred lies about Bolivar's intentions. Plots were discovered in Mexico hatched under the influence of the United States. There was a universal feeling in South America that this first-born republic, which ought to have helped the younger ones, was, on the contrary, only trying to encourage discord and to foment difficulties so as to intervene at the appropriate moment.

Informed of these attempts, but powerless against this unexpected opponent, Bolivar began to realize that peace would not necessarily bring tranquillity to his country.

XLIII

THE first republic to fall a prey to grave dissensions was Venezuela.

Returning to Bogotá, Bolivar concentrated troops there, for the situation threatened to grow worse; he proclaimed a state of siege in several departments and took the field, desirous to avoid bloodshed as much as possible, but also desirous to reëstablish order.

From Coro, Bolivar wrote to General Paez, who was among the most dangerous malcontents at Caracas:

'I have read with satisfaction your proclamation to Valencia. Would to Heaven that your hopes could be realized! My one desire is the welfare of Venezuela and at the same time of all America. I can assure you that I am weary of the life which I lead, and that I shall not be happy until my resignation is accepted by the great Convention. Then my true feelings will be known to the world.

'I fear a descent from the heights to which the fate of my country has raised my fame. I have never wished for power; it is toilsome to me, odious, and I will do nothing to retain it. I have even come to hope for death, which when it comes will deliver me from these complications. But Colombia fills my mind: I see our work destroyed and the curses of generations falling upon us, as those responsible for the chaos.

There is but one road to lead us from this abyss; that of duty.

'I remain at the head of Colombia because the national vote has called me there. Who, then, shall snatch my power from me? Your friends, yourself? Ingratitude is more contemptible than treason; I will not believe in such baseness.

'It is impossible, General, that you should wish to see me humiliated by a pack of cowards whom we never saw upon the battle-field. Do not dishonour Caracas by making her a centre of infamy.

'Without the services that I have given, the dangers that I have braved, my victories, my perseverance, neither you, General, nor any one, would have the position that you have to-day nor the glory which surrounds you.

'You wish to see in me only a plain citizen. The title would flatter me in other circumstances, but just now I have come back from Peru on purpose to avoid a civil war.

'Venezuela at this moment must recognize no authority but mine.

'The mandate which you hold from the municipalities is the result of three murders, which is scarcely pleasant for such a man as you.

'Are you, yes or no, disposed to obey me, and Venezuela to recognize me as her leader?

'If need be I will fight against you all; it will be the sixth civil war that I have had to suppress.

'What more can I say to you than this?

'I am ready to summon the National Convention, and so that no one can accuse me of favouring any party I will leave Colombia: the best proof of this is the sale of my property which my sister is in the act of negotiating.

'I will await your reply at Puerto Cabello, a town still full of your renown. I hope that you will act so honourably that it will remain untarnished.'

At Puerto Cabello, Bolivar received no word of Paez. He merely heard that the latter had been very uneasy at the reported arrival of the Liberator's troops. Bolivar wrote again to Paez:

'If I bring my soldiers with me, I have reasons for acting thus. Venezuela is a prey to discord. I know that there are plots against my life. Guzman, who is your friend as well as mine, has just escaped assassination. At San Francisco my patriotism is insulted; at Valencia, where you are, vile proclamations are posted up in my name. Since you are unable to enforce my authority in the territory which I have commissioned you to govern, I am coming in person to make myself respected. If you make war on the Republic, so much the worse for you, but I will never permit the sacrifice of those who have done their duty.

'We can blame ourselves for many things, but you cannot accuse me of being a party to the troubles of Venezuela. If I have come here, it is brought by you. No slightest ambition has moved me. I have but now

once more refused the dictatorship which they wished
to restore to me.

'As I have told you, I desire to avoid all civil war,
and I will give way before a National Convention at
which I will not even be present.

'Let us unite to save our brothers.

'What! You whom I have loved as my dearest
friend; how could you be thus led away?

'You ruin us in ruining yourself.

'Come and see me. What can you fear from me?
I went alone to meet Morillo, who brought his cavalry
with him. I have no wish to be avenged on you. If
you are afraid to come yourself, send a deputy. We
ought to come to an understanding, for the situation
is both sad and dangerous.'

XLIV

By Bolivar's orders Paez was dismissed from his civil and military offices and accused of treason. The town of Valencia took the part of Paez, who became the real leader of the insurrection. Without wasting an instant, Bolivar marched on Caracas, where, however, he was received with enthusiasm. They felt him to be the stronger man, and he seemed determined to take the most radical measures. Paez sent General Silva to him to set forth his claims. A majority of Venezuelans demanded the partition of Colombia; New Granada and Venezuela would remain on very good terms, but it was in the interests of all that they asked for this separation.

Bolivar replied:

'You will say to General Paez that I am glad to see his return to better feelings. As for the partition of Colombia, the question has already been laid before the Congress at Bogotá; but I have not the necessary power to settle this difference. The Assembly will deal with it.'

Paez made overtures to the Liberator, promising to do his best to appease the malcontents, but he did not dare to go to Bolivar, whose ill-will he feared. He felt himself to blame, and the Liberator was obliged to make him ashamed of his fears by announcing that he would come alone to Valencia to interview him.

In spite of all, Paez was a warrior and could not

forget what he owed to Bolivar, whose genius and honesty he was forced to admit. He had let himself be dragged into a revolt of which he was by no means proud and of which in the bottom of his heart he disapproved. As Mariño had formerly done at Cumaná, he assembled his officers, addressed proclamations to the people of Valencia pledging them to give the Liberator the triumphal entry which had been voted after the victories in Peru. He even went so far as to demand to be brought before the court-martial at Bogotá for his conduct.

Bolivar displayed his magnanimity; he went to Paez and thanked him for having, while there was yet time, saved the country by his action. He refused to impeach Paez before a court. In the joy of having been able to save the lives of his compatriots, he wished to forget what had passed.

In his satisfaction he pushed kindness to the point of weakness. He forbade the printers to publish anything whatsoever to recall the dissensions, of which he never wished to hear again. He gave proof of so much generosity towards his late enemies, confirmed them in their former offices and loaded them with such benefits, that those who had never been traitors took umbrage and accused the Liberator of rewarding the men who had been ready to fight against him more generously than those who had always upheld him.

Bolivar was still reproached for having made a republic of Upper Peru, while the Argentine had claims on several departments. But in forming Bolivia the

Liberator had hoped to put a buffer between the Peruvians and the Argentines, who hated each other. He was also accused of having secretly negotiated the division of South America with the Emperor of Brazil. The treaty was quite a different thing and consisted only of a definition of the Bolivian frontiers.

Sucre, who was struggling among terrible complications, wrote often to Bolivar to ask his advice. Civil dissensions followed one another. Buenos Ayres demanded the province of Tarija; Peru would not hear of it. Sucre made the decisions which his honesty dictated to him, but he was inundated by manifold jealousies. He had only accepted the Presidency for two years, and he was longing to retire. He was re-elected for two years more. Anarchy was lying in wait for Bolivia, and Bolivar, who always felt a weakness for this republic, which he called his pet daughter, tried to persuade Sucre to do his best to stand against these troubles. He wrote:

'Your country is less to be pitied than Venezuela, where the poverty is becoming terrible. The people have not yet returned to work with any heart; they have suffered too long and have lost the taste for labour. The ambition, hatred, and unscrupulousness of the highest officials, the hardships, the attempts at civil war, have led my country to a very sad pass.'

XLV

José de Sucre, sickened by the hypocrisy and ambition of the magistrates, sent in his resignation, in spite of his love for his Bolivian fatherland, which bore the name of the Liberator and whose capital bore his own name. He was disgusted with the Presidency and retired into Colombia. At once there was anarchy. All the lawyers and officers who had been watching for Sucre's departure quarrelled over the succession.

In Peru, a Congress called to consider the Bolivian Constitution, with a view to its adoption, rejected it unanimously. Marshal Don José de Lamar was elected President of Peru in place of Bolivar: he invaded Bolivian territory under the pretext of preventing that nation from having a constitution which Peru would by no means accept.

In New Granada, Cartagena, Ocaña, and Magdalena were in a state of open civil war. The violent action of two of Bolivar's colonels in a printer's shop was made an excuse for insulting articles upon the Liberator. The majority of the Congress were no longer, as formerly, for Bolivar; they demanded explanations of his most trifling acts. On the other hand, a public meeting invited Bolivar to dissolve the Congress, and to resume the supreme command until peace should be established everywhere. It was a new dictatorship which the Liberator, desirous of peace, accepted from the people. But Bolivar was no longer the hero of Liberty; folk bore him a grudge, and every day he was more openly accused of retaining power against the will of the Congress.

Two plots against his person came to light.

He faced every difficulty and gave himself no rest, no longer even considering his health; he felt the situation to be full of danger and needed to act with decision. Every measure roused discontent. Santander, the Vice-President, was jealous of Bolivar and tried to sap his power; he hid his selfish designs beneath a cloak of pure patriotism, and in that blindly prejudiced country he recruited enthusiastic partisans.

Secret societies were formed all over Colombia, which were to have branches in every important town. At a given signal a meeting was to be organized to protest against the reactionary dictatorship; there was to be a demand for a new parliament to put an end to Bolivar's despotism. Military mutinies were to be carefully prepared in the garrisons.

But Santander was in no hurry; he knew that a majority of the army was still for the Liberator, and he feared that by precipitating matters he might lead to the ruin of his plans. He had accepted the post of envoy to the United States, and preferred to wait till he was there before putting the spark to the explosion. If the insurrection miscarried, the responsibility would be diverted from him and he could choose another time.

On September 24th, an accusation brought about the arrest of a certain officer. It happened that the colonel whose duty it was to inquire into the affair was one of the conspirators; he thought it an excellent opportunity; any longer delay and the truth might become known. He postponed his so-called inquiry till the next day; that night he summoned a dozen conspirators and twenty-five soldiers, and decided to assassinate the Dictator without delay.

The conspirators arrived before the house where Bolivar was living. A soldier asked for a light for his cigar, and in the instant of giving it the sentinel was stabbed in the back.

Bolivar's mistress, Manuela Saenz, had not yet gone to bed; she heard the fall of a body in the street and looked out of the window. She saw a crowd; at once she shut the door which led to the staircase and awakened her lover. As there was no doubt about the intentions of the people in the street, they both escaped into the passage, leaving the house from the other side with the help of a rope.

Bolivar was scarcely dressed; he ran to arouse a police post, and at the head of about fifty men took the plotters by surprise while they were still in the act of searching for him. The conspirators were arrested, disarmed, and put under guard in the salon of the very house they had come to attack. Unluckily, they had had time to murder Colonel Ferguson, who slept in an adjoining room.

At the other end of the town a detachment of artillery had risen and had seized the prison buildings. General Padilla, whom Bolivar had imprisoned a few days earlier, was set at liberty. Bolivar's brother Joseph was basely killed. A squadron of cavalry retook the prison, and two hours later the insurrection had been extinguished.

All night long in the market-place Bolivar examined the prisoners. One of them had given a list of the conspirators, and none had been able to escape.

At break of day fourteen of them were shot; the others were sentenced to imprisonment. Santander, who was seriously implicated in the affair, was condemned to death. He was degraded in the presence of the whole army. Bolivar generously commuted his penalty to perpetual banishment, and gave Paez the duty of seeing that he left Colombia. Paez, who hated Santander, began by shutting him up for seven months in the cells at Bocachica before he gave him a passport to Europe.

Bolivar prohibited all the Masonic lodges, veritable hotbeds of conspiracy. Secret societies were forbidden. The universities, which were becoming centres of opposition, were closed. Bolivar revised the list of studies and excluded every branch that might, among feather-headed young people, give rise to ideas harmful to the commonweal. They were replaced by the history of the Catholic religion, and additional courses in Latin and Canon Law.

For a moment Bolivar had thought of finally leaving Colombia, and of pardoning all the culprits, but the disastrous experience of the former effects of his kindness made him for once lay aside his generosity and use unrelenting rigour against those who in attacking his person attacked also the liberty of the country.

XLVI

IN the province of Popayan, Colonels J. M. Obando and J. H. Lopez rose with their troops and declared war on Bolivar. This was a serious menace, for the colonels were very able officers, and the district of Popayan was mountainous and well adapted for guerrilla warfare. Against these rebels Bolivar despatched General Flores, who succeeded in defeating them and pursued them as far as the Peruvian frontier.

Peru welcomed the rebels, espoused their cause, imprisoned a Colombian Minister, occupied two provinces, sent an ambassador to Bogotá, and refused to pay the sums due from the Government at Lima for the expenses of the Colombian intervention in 1823.

On July 3d, Bolivar declared war on Peru.

Marshal Lamar replied to him by proclaiming a blockade of the Colombian ports on the Pacific coast. A Peruvian squadron, comprising a frigate, a corvette, and three brigs, bombarded Guayaquil, broke the boom, burned the fort at Cruces, and destroyed several fishing boats. At the same time Lamar invaded Colombia with nine thousand men. Sucre marched to meet him and defeated him several times.

Obando and Lopez had resumed hostilities. Bolivar sent Cordoba and Heres against them, promising an amnesty if they would lay down their arms at once.

The two colonels accepted. Lamar, vanquished by Sucre, signed an armistice which he broke a week later and again took the offensive. Bolivar sent orders to his West Indian fleet to round Cape Horn and return by the Pacific. The Peruvian frigate at Guayaquil was sunk, the port retaken, Lamar was deposed by a revolution, and peace was signed on September 22d.

Peru undertook to restore the ships and materials of war which she had seized, to demobilize, to pay her debts of 1823–24, and to respect the former frontier.

Peru and Colombia decided on the abolition of slavery and the punishment as pirates of all who practised this trade. All disputes were to be settled by the arbitration of Chile.

General Cordoba, after having beaten the rebels in the province of Popayan, himself revolted. The Irishman O'Leary was sent to oppose him. He hurried down the stream of the Magdalena, and at Santurio engaged him in a terribly sanguinary battle in which Cordoba was killed.

Calm seemed to be reëstablished. The populace, who desired peace, wished for a monarchy, of which Bolivar would have been the first king. A strong government was more than ever needed to resist those who made a profit from disorder. Bolivar had still some illusions as to the feelings of his compatriots. Above all things he dreaded to appear in the world's eyes as a tyrant. He refused the crown and waited impatiently for the 2d of January, 1830, the end of his dictatorship. Power suddenly alarmed him. He was afraid of being suspected of the slightest ambition.

XLVII

ONE Sunday, as he was coming out of church Bolivar
stumbled and fell. He had difficulty in rising; they
carried him home. For several days he remained in
bed, feeling very weak. He looked at himself in a
glass and was startled by his appearance; his cheeks
were hollow, he was emaciated, his hair had turned
white. He was only forty-six years old. Was he to die
before he had secured the happiness of his people?
He had a sudden foreboding of it.

Several times he asked for Marshal Sucre. He was
told that Sucre was on a journey, very far away.
Realizing that something was being kept from him, he
besought Manuela to tell him the whole truth. He
learned that Sucre had just been assassinated.

Bolivar had not even the strength to weep; he remained motionless, stricken down by grief.

The scoundrels, the bandits, they had killed the
cleanest, the most honest, the most admirable of men!

XLVIII

FROM Mexico to Cape Horn there was civil war.

In Peru no one, not even Lamar, had been able to replace Bolivar. One President succeeded another; it was a game of grab; the highest officials quarrelled over the most puerile questions. When the papers were not full of odious and lying propaganda, they were mere lists of crimes. Fifty different parties were at deadly war; none of them could come to the front without being immediately attacked by another even more fierce.

Anarchy reigned at Guatemala; there was neither President nor Ministers; colonels at the head of brigands ravaged the country, made laws as it pleased them, and the people were ruined and driven from their homes.

Mexico was governed by mere bandits, who held foreigners to ransom, plundered churches, and hanged their enemies without trial. The elections were made at the point of the pistol. Two opponents fought a terrible battle; suddenly taking fright as to the issue of the combat they fled, each his own way, abandoning their followers to the struggle. The *rabonas* or *vivanderas* fought even more savagely than their husbands. In the evening the victorious party had the greatest difficulty in recovering their leader, who was already far away. Nothing happened straightforwardly. All the communications were interrupted;

the coaches dared not venture themselves upon the roads. Bands of thieves set free from prison allied themselves with their own guards to plunder the villages.

At Buenos Ayres they had no longer to deal with that Liniers who with two hundred ragamuffins recaptured the town from the English and protected the country against every one. The *gauchos* of the Pampas, the Indians of Patagonia, who knew now that you cannot stop a cannon-ball with a hat, were the terror of the towns. Generals set out with two thousand men to put down the troubles, and if they came back they came alone; all the soldiers had deserted and formed themselves into robber bands to seek their fortunes.

Indians threatened the suburbs of Buenos Ayres. No longer a single noble figure, but officers who seized upon immense territories had themselves made Presidents and exercised a scoundrelly dictatorship.

There were no workers in the mines or in the fields, commerce was ruined, and foreign vessels no longer called at the ports.

As for Colombia, she was no better than the rest,

XLIX

Riots broke out here and there.

At Caracas it was decreed that Venezuela should be separated from New Granada; that Bolivar was no longer at the head of the Government; that Paez should hold power as long as the uncertainty lasted.

Thus the Liberator's resignation was now not only unopposed; it was forced upon him.

Bolivar had refused the throne; so be it, it is what his friends had expected from him. Was he sincere when he accepted power only with reluctance?

Paez tried to govern without too much treachery to his benefactor, but also without displeasing his supporters. At a lucky moment he had bought all the paper money of his officers and men for next to nothing, and then sold it to them again after the victory. He was immensely rich and his sudden fortune had intoxicated him. He was for the partition of Colombia, but he wished to avoid abuses.

If the people had no longer the least respect for Bolivar, in a short time they would have no respect for himself. He tried to bring this too forgetful populace back to better feelings; he defended Bolivar, showed how straightforward and fine his conduct had always been, and promised to uphold his cause. Meanwhile, he advised Bolivar not to oppose the reforms which he himself suggested.

An English admiral, Sir Charles E. Fleming, interfered in all Venezuelan affairs; he wanted to have the law against slavery abolished, and, as he knew that Bolivar would refuse, he offered considerable sums to Paez to oppose the Liberator.

On the 15th of January, 1830, not more than half the deputies were present at the meeting of the great Congress. Bolivar addressed a touching proclamation to the people:

'I have served you these twenty years as statesman and soldier; we have liberated our country and three republics and put down many civil wars.

'My only pride has been to direct your courage and your patriotism.

'All those who envy me my position have tried to spread slanders, to credit me with their own designs. I have been unworthily suspected. I have never had the intention of reigning.

'My one desire has been to protect you, to win respect for our dear-bought freedom.

'Listen to me for the last time. I renounce any political career, but I beseech you to remain united, do not be your own executioners in the murder of your country.'

The new President, Joaquin Mosquera, who was an honest man, had the following decree voted:

'Seeing that Bolivar has devoted his life and his wealth to the service of Colombia, that his exploits have called forth the admiration of the whole world,

BED-ALCOVE IN WHICH BOLIVAR WAS BORN

that he has been a powerful help to the cause of South America, that during his whole existence he has given proof of magnificent self-sacrifice, the Liberator has every right to a demonstration of the national gratitude.

'The Congress now sitting presents to the Liberator Simon Bolivar, in the name of the Colombian fatherland, the tribute of her eternal thankfulness.

'Into whatever part of the Republic he retires, he shall have a right to the respect due to her greatest citizen.

'The Executive power allocates to the Liberator an annuity of 30,000 piastres.

'Bogotá. *May 9, 1830.*'

But not a piastre did Bolivar ever receive, for the simple reason that the Treasury was empty, that the taxes were not paid, and that those in charge of the finances — whether they were called Paez or Arismendi — helped themselves first, that the army was reduced to the ordinary ration, and that the pensions to the victims of the war had not been paid for a long time.

Bolivar was no more than a plain citizen. Yesterday he had still been feared; to-day he was insulted. Paez went so far as to write that, the country seeing in Bolivar the great cause of all its misfortunes, it was impossible to begin negotiations as long as Bolivar had not left Colombian territory.

Venezuela separated itself finally from New Granada, which alone kept the name of Colombia in memory of a glorious past.

President Mosquera had much difficulty in repressing the troubles fomented by General Jimenez. After much parleying, even the Government troops revolted. Jimenez marched quietly to Bogotá and took it without difficulty. Mosquera gave in his resignation.

Once more Bolivar was to be recalled from his retirement and asked to intervene.

When anarchy had brought them to the most desperate pass, people remembered the Liberator, and once again Bolivar, forgetting all his grievances and the illness which more and more tormented him, left his resting-place and put himself at the head of the nation.

He still had strength to address these words to the Colombian people:

'I promise to serve my country as a citizen and as a soldier.

'I will sacrifice everything to be able to tell the world that Colombia is peaceful, respected, flourishing, and happy.'

On September 22, 1830, the town of Cartagena appointed Bolivar supreme head of the Republic.

But the provinces were not all pacified, some were threatening. The provisional government ordered the formation of an army of six thousand men to meet the first necessities.

Every man waited anxiously for the return of the Liberator.

L

But Bolivar could no longer dash from one town to another or spring to horse to subdue rebels eight hundred miles away. He was worn out.

On the 16th of October he wrote to General Urdaneta:

'My health is more and more affected, for I suffer from several diseases at the same time. My liver is greatly inflamed, and at times I experience nervous spasms; added to that, the rheumatism which I thought was cured has returned. If I nurse one malady, the others suffer for it. The heat is bad for my liver, the damp disastrous to my rheumatism. I cannot walk without terrible pain; going upstairs is out of the question, I am seized with giddiness. The slightest draught makes me ill, and in spite of the high temperature here, I am dressed in wool from head to foot.

'Why do I trouble you with these annoyances?

'The worst of it is that I have no doctor and that the climate here is certainly unfavourable to me. I should like a voyage, perhaps seasickness would do me good.

'Medicines disgust me; in spite of all my suffering, I cannot make up my mind to take them.

'You will realize, my dear General, that I cannot keep my promise. It is impossible for me to resume power. How can I help this nation when I have no longer even the strength to stand upright? Being no more good for anything, I am reduced to taking care of what remains of my miserable carcase.

'Exercise the Presidency in my place, or appoint some one whom you think capable of that duty.

'I hope that in a week I shall be better and able to go to Santa Marta. The baths could do me no harm. After all, what do I know about it? Perhaps the régime that I am following is the exact opposite of that I ought to observe. I have no doctor to advise me.

'Farewell, my dear General. I can dictate no longer. I am choked with fits of coughing.'

On the 1st of December, 1830, Bolivar arrived at Santa Marta. His friends could scarcely recognize him. He could no longer walk; they carried him as far as a little house to which they summoned a French physician, Dr. Reverend.

A shipowner, Joaquin Mier, had offered his vessel to take Bolivar to Jamaica, where the waters of the Blue Mountains might perhaps do him good. But any movement might be fatal to the Liberator. The project was abandoned.

One night Bolivar began to rave:

'Let us go, let us go! These people do not want us here, my soldiers will follow me. We must hurry and carry my things on to the frigate; I can stay no longer. Ah! my lads! . . .'

During the day Bolivar recovered his senses a little. He spoke to his doctor:

'And you, Doctor, what did you come to seek in this country?'

'Freedom.'

'You found it?'

'Yes, General.'

'Well, you are more fortunate than I. Go back to France, where I should like to accompany you. There is too much of a rabble here.'

A priest was summoned, a simple village curé who came to bring the last Sacraments.

Bolivar made his will and dictated his last farewell to his nation:

'I wish for the happiness of my country. If my death can bring an end to discord I shall go down happy to the tomb.'

But he turned towards Dr. Reverend:

'Yes, to the tomb. That is what they have brought me to. Ah, if only it could be of any use . . .'

These were his last words. He lost consciousness, and his death agony lasted till one o'clock on the 17th of December, when he died.

A few friends and some poor Indians followed the funeral. To meet the expenses of the ceremony it was necessary to borrow money from the neighbours, who gave it with very ill grace.

INDEX

DATE DUE